101

FAMILY DAYS OUT

WITH THE NATIONAL TRUST 2007

THE NATIONAL TRUST

First published in Great Britain by National Trust Books
An imprint of Anova Books

Text copyright © The National Trust, 2007
Design and layout copyright © National Trust Books, 2007
Image copyright © National Trust Picture Library

The moral rights of the author and photographers have been asserted

ISBN-10 1905400470
ISBN-13 9781905400478

A CIP catalogue record for this book is available from the British Library.

Designed by Lee-May Lim and Mark Holt

10 9 8 7 6 5 4 3 2 1

Colour Reproduction by Anorax Imaging Limited, UK
Printed in China by WKT Co Ltd

The Publisher is committed to respecting the intellectual property rights of others. We have therefore taken all reasonable efforts to ensure that the reproduction of all content on these pages is done with the full consent of copyright owners. If you are aware of any unintentional omissions please contact the company directly so that any necessary corrections may be made for future editions.

All photographs by NTPL except 97 x 2: NT/John Willis. NTPL: 136 (bottom), 147. Matthew Antrobus: 8, 15, 23, 52, 77, 113, 123, 124, 135, 139. Bill Batten: 65,133. Andrew Butler: 19, 20, 32, 44/5, 46, 80, 89,107, 125, 140,141. Michael Caldwell: 10, 94, 145,146. Joe Cornish: 17,18, 50 (top), 50 (bottom), 51 (bottom), 83 (top), 83 (bottom), 111, 112, 121, 129, 132, 152, 153,155. Derek Croucher: 35, 38, 41, 47, 54,154. Will Curwen: 134. Rod J. Edwards: 74, Andreas von Einsiedel: 34, 37, 57, 75, 88, 90, 92, 93, 102, 103,104,130,138, 143, 150, 157. Geoffrey Frosh: 42, 43, 109. Lee Frost: 127. Chris Gascoigne: 24. Dennis Gilbert: 106, 114. John Hammond: 122,142. Jerry Harpur: 33. Paul Harris: 91. Andrew Haslam: 99. Nigel Hicks: 36. Angelo Hornak: 70. Andrea Jones: 39, 40. Chris King: 66,105. David Levenson: 21, 22, 25, 69, 81,126,160 (top right),160 (bottom left). Nadia Mackenzie: 27, 117. Leo Mason: 49, 51 (top), 71. Nick Meers: 98, 100, 101, 101,110, 148. John Miller: 137 (top). David Noton: 16, 26, 96. Stephen Robson: 2, 29, 40, 59, 62, 108, 118, 119. Ian Shaw: 1,13, 28, 30, 31, 48, 58, 61, 67, 68, 82 (bottom), 84, 85, 86, 95, 136 (top), 144, 149, 151,156. Geraint Tellem: 137 (bottom). Rupert Truman: 64, 76, 116. Charlie Waite: 85. Paul Wakefield: 72, 73, 82 (top),128. Ian West: 56, 60. J. Whitaker: 120. Andy Williams: 55. Mike Williams: 79, 115, 131. Jennie Woodcock: 53, 63, 87,160 (top left), 160 (bottom right), 160 (bottom centre).

Information correct at time of going to press. Please check with the property before making a long journey.

Contents

Places to visit

South West

1 Arlington Court
2 Avebury
3 Brownsea Island
4 Buckland Abbey
5 Castle Drogo
6 Chedworth Roman Villa
7 Corfe Castle
8 Cornish Mines & Engines
9 Dunster Castle
10 Dyrham Park
11 Finch Foundry
12 Glendurgan Garden
13 Killerton
14 Lanhydrock
15 Lydford Gorge
16 Overbeck's
17 Saltram House
18 St Michael's Mount
19 Trelissick Garden

South & South East

20 Ashridge Estate
21 Bateman's
22 Bodiam Castle
23 Box Hill
24 Claremont Landscape Garden
25 Dapdune Wharf & River Wey
26 Devil's Dyke, The
27 Hughenden Manor
28 Ightham Mote
29 Needles Old Battery
30 Petworth House
31 Polesden Lacey
32 Sheffield Park Garden
33 Witley & Milford Commons

London & East of England

34 Belton House
35 Blickling Hall, Garden & Park
36 Dunstable Downs
37 Dunwich Heath & Beach
38 Ham House
39 Hatfield Forest
40 Houghton Mill
41 Ickworth House & Park
42 Morden Hall Park & Snuff Mill
43 Osterley Park
44 Oxburgh Hall
45 Sutton Hoo
46 Sutton House
47 Tattershall Castle
48 Wicken Fen
49 Wimpole Home Farm
50 Woolsthorpe Manor

Central

51 Attingham Park
52 Baddesley Clinton
53 Berrington Hall
54 Brockhampton Estate
55 Calke Abbey
56 Charlecote Park
57 Clumber Park
58 Croome Park
59 Hardwick Hall
60 Kedleston Hall
61 Shugborough Estate
62 Snowshill Manor
63 Sudbury Hall
64 Workhouse, The

North West

65 Beatrix Potter Gallery
66 Dunham Massey
67 Fell Foot Park
68 Formby
69 Lyme Park
70 Quarry Bank Mill & Styal Estate
71 Rufford Old Hall
72 Speke Hall
73 Wordsworth House

North East

74 Beningbrough Hall & Gardens
75 Brimham Rocks
76 Cherryburn
77 East Riddlesden Hall
78 Fountains Abbey & Studley Hall
79 Gibside
80 Hadrian's Wall & Housestead's Fort
81 Hardcastle Crags
82 Nostell Priory
83 Nunnington Hall
84 Souter Lighthouse
85 Treasurer's House
86 Wallington

Wales* & Northern Ireland

87 Chirk Castle*
88 Dinefwr Park*
89 Dolaucothi Gold Mines*
90 Erdigg*
91 Llanerchaeron*
92 Penrhyn Castle*
93 Plas Newydd*
94 Powis Castle & Gardens*
95 Argory, The
96 Castle Ward & Strangford Loch
97 Crom Estate
98 Florence Court
99 Giant's Causeway
100 Mount Stewart House
101 Springhill & Wellbrook Beetling Mill

Introduction

101 Family Days Out with the National Trust is for anyone who'd like to find a fun and educational place to visit.

At each of our specially selected properties – historic houses, castles, gardens or beautiful stretches of coast and countryside – the whole family will find all kinds of things of interest to see and do.

There are so many places in the care of the National Trust that have so much to offer to families, but, as we can't cram them all in this book, we've chosen some of our particular favourites. The wonderful thing is you never know what interest you might awaken in your children – or yourself – with a visit to a National Trust property! From rare birds, insects, farm animals, statues, dolls' houses, mazes and mills to mines, children's lives in past times, life 'below stairs' … the list is endless. Or you may all simply enjoy having an invigorating day out in the open air, making the most of the glorious countryside that the National Trust protects and cares for. There's something for the whole family in every region. More ideas for great days out in your local area can be found on our website: www.nationaltrust.org.uk.

For more information about joining the National Trust, please visit our website (you can join online), ring 0870 458 4000, or email enquiries@thenationaltrust.org.uk.

How to use this book

What to see

As well as drawing attention to fabulous views and features, this section includes things to look out for of particular interest to children. They often highlight quirky things such as secret priest's holes and gruesome creatures carved into woodwork, which are not always what the place is best known for.

What to do

This gives suggestions for what children and families can do at each property – again, often including features such as grassy slopes to run down – and activities especially designed for children. These take place usually, but not exclusively, in the school holidays and can range from butter-making in the Tudor kitchen at Buckland Abbey to pond dipping at Wicken Fen. There is sometimes a very small extra charge for these activities which are run as part of the Trust's commitment to informal education. Please contact individual properties for details of activities.

Special events

Entries under this heading tend to include larger, one-off events such as a teddy bears' picnic at Castle Ward or Apple Days at Sir Isaac Newton's house. There will often be a charge for entry and any one event can attract thousands of families. Events are mainly held in the summer holidays but many properties run Halloween and Christmas events and Easter egg hunts sponsored by Sky in 2007. Events will, of course, change every year and those included for each entry are a taster only. Please contact individual properties for this information or check the Events section on the NT website: www.nationaltrust.org.uk.

By the way...

This section includes any extra information that families may find particularly useful, such as baby-changing facilities, or children's menus, or details of accessibility. Please note that the guide's information was correct at the time of going to press, but please do check before your trip. If you have questions you should contact the property concerned.

Things to Know Before Visiting

Admission prices

Admission prices vary, so check the current National Trust Handbook or the National Trust website for the latest details: www.nationaltrust.org.uk or ring 0870 458 4000.

A family ticket usually allows two adults and up to three children to visit all sections of a property (e.g. house, garden, museum, etc.) for a set price. Costs may vary considerably.

Buying National Trust family membership may be good value if you plan to visit several National Trust properties over the year. Under 5s are admitted free unless other conditions apply, and children aged 5-16 usually pay half the adult entry price. Many properties offer special educational facilities and programmes. Please ring 0870 458 4000 or contact the property directly for more information (see p. 159 for membership details).

Busy properties

Properties can be extremely popular at bank holidays and summer weekends. At some properties, timed tickets may be in operation to smooth the flow of visitors to avoid overcrowding.

Learning and discovery

The National Trust is committed to learning and providing experiences that are inspiring, stimulating and fun. Over 60 National Trust properties have children's guides; many others have tracker packs to help children understand the houses and gardens or special trails or objects that can be handled. Please ring ahead of your visit to find out what each property has to offer. Please have a peek at www.nationaltrust.org.uk/learning for details of activities and events for a fabulous day out.

Shopping and eating

The National Trust runs restaurants, shops, tea-rooms and holiday cottages to fund the Trust's work. Each purchase makes a vital contribution to this work. Many properties have shops offering a wide range of related merchandise, much of which is exclusive to the Trust. Our restaurants and tea-rooms offer a welcoming atmosphere, value for money and traditional home cooking, with many properties featuring menus with a historical theme, often cooked with local and seasonal produce.

Picnics

Many properties welcome picnics and some have designated areas. If you are planning a picnic at a Trust property, please phone in advance to check. Fires and barbecues are not usually allowed (sorry!)

Facilities for young families

Many properties provide baby-feeding and changing areas, sometimes in purpose-designed parent and baby rooms. Restaurants have highchairs, children's menus, colouring sheets and in some cases, play areas. Staff are very happy to advise you about what is on offer.

In historic buildings, visitors with small babies are welcome to use front slings, which are often available on loan; hip-carrying infant seats or reins for toddlers can also be borrowed from selected places. There are usually arrangements for storing prams or pushchairs at the entrance, as it is not possible to take these into fragile areas. Some houses can admit baby back-carriers at all times, while in others, it will be up to the discretion of staff, depending on how busy the property may be. We understand that the restrictions on back-carriers, prams and pushchairs may be awkward for those with older and/or heavier children, and as access arrangements vary at each property, we suggest that you telephone in advance for details of any restrictions. We have tried to include some details of access arrangements for each place to visit.

And before you go

To avoid disappointment, we suggest phoning ahead to check that a property is going to be open, or an activity is definitely on, or is not booked up – events get very busy in the holidays or on summer weekends. And remember that events are always being organised, especially in the summer holidays, the Christmas and Easter seasons and other school breaks. Go to the website and check the property you want to visit – there's a section for 'events', or give them a call to see what they have planned.

National Trust contacts

National Trust Membership Department, PO Box 39, Warrington WA5 7WD
Tel: 0870 458 4000 Minicom: 0870 240 3207; www.nationaltrust.org.uk
Email enquiries@thenationaltrust.org.uk for all general enquiries including membership and requests for information. Please note that the phones are manned 9:00am–5:30pm Monday to Friday and 9:00am–4:00pm weekends and public holidays.

Central Office
The National Trust & National Trust (Enterprises) Ltd, Heelis, Kemble Drive, Swindon, Wiltshire SN2 2NA
Tel: 01793 817400; www.nationaltrust.org.uk

National Trust Regional Offices

✉ **Devon & Cornwall**
Cornwall: Lanhydrock, Bodmin PL30 4DE Tel: 01208 74281
Devon: Killerton House, Broadclyst, Exeter EX5 3LE Tel: 01392 881691
✉ **Wessex (Bristol, Bath, Dorset, Gloucestershire, Somerset & Wiltshire)**
Eastleigh Court, Bishopstrow, Warminster, Wiltshire BA12 9HW Tel: 01985 843600
✉ **Thames & Solent (Berkshire, Buckinghamshire, Hampshire, part of Hertfordshire, Isle of Wight, Greater London & Oxfordshire)**
Hughenden Manor, High Wycombe, Buckinghamshire HP14 4LA Tel: 01494 528051
✉ **South East (Sussex, Kent, Surrey)**
Polesden Lacey, Dorking, Surrey RH5 6BD Tel: 01372 453401
✉ **East of England (Bedfordshire, Cambridgeshire, Essex, part of Hertfordshire, Norfolk & Suffolk)**
Westley Bottom, Bury St Edmunds, Suffolk IP33 3WD Tel: 01284 747500
✉ **East Midlands (Derbyshire, Leicestershire, South Lincolnshire, Northamptonshire, Nottinghamshire & Rutland)**
Clumber Park Stableyard, Worksop, Nottinghamshire S80 3BE Tel: 01909 486411
✉ **West Midlands (Birmingham, Herefordshire, Shropshire, Staffordshire, Warwickshire & Worcestershire)**
Attingham Park, Shrewsbury, Shropshire SY4 4TP Tel: 01743 708100
✉ **North West**
Cumbria: The Hollens, Grasmere, Ambleside, Cumbria LA22 9QZ
Tel: 0870 6095391
Cheshire, Greater Manchester, Lancashire & Merseyside: Stamford Estates, 18 Market Street, Altrincham, Cheshire WA14 1PH Tel: 0161 928 0075
✉ **Yorkshire & North East**
Yorkshire, Teeside, North Lincolnshire: Goddards, 27 Tadcaster Road, Dringhouses, York YO24 1GG
Tel: 01904 702021
County Durham, Newcastle & Tyneside & Northumberland: Scots' Gap, Morpeth, Northumberland NE61 4EG
Tel: 01670 774691

National Trust Office for Wales
Trinity Square, Llandudno LL30 2DE Tel: 01492 860123

National Trust Office for Northern Ireland
Rowallane House, Saintfield, Ballynahinch, County Down BT24 7LH Tel: 028 9751 0721

The National Trust for Scotland (separate organization)
Wemyss House, 28 Charlotte Square, Edinburgh EH2 4ET Tel: 0131 243 9300 www.nts.org.uk

Symbols

Playground or play area

Picnic area

Animals. This means children can see wild or other animals while on a visit. For instance, this symbol is shown for Wimpole Home Farm. It is also included if there are significant numbers of animals such as squirrels, deer or sheep in parkland around houses, or on other parts of a property.

Quiz sheet, trail sheet or children's guide. Many properties have fun quiz sheets, trails or guidebooks especially written for children. These cost from just 25p to £2–3 at ticket points or in National Trust shops at individual properties. Some are free. They are generally written in a child-friendly style and will greatly enhance a child's experience of a property.

Café or restaurant

Children's menu. Toys in restaurant. Highchairs in restaurant. These three symbols relate to practical provision for families in the café or restaurant. Where toys are indicated, these range from Trusty colouring sheets through robust table-top toys. Bottle warming can be arranged on request. The National Trust is constantly aiming to improve in this area and most properties now offer children's menus and high chairs.

Wheelchair access. This symbol indicates that a reasonable amount of the property can be enjoyed from a wheelchair without undue difficulty. Outside, wheelchair-friendly areas are likely to be suitable for pushchairs too; for instance, where boardwalks or paths are smooth and flat.

Shop

Dogs on leads in park and garden. Except for guide dogs and hearing dogs, dogs are not allowed into Trust houses, restaurants and gardens. This symbol means dogs are allowed on a lead in parkland. In countryside areas it is advisable to keep your dog on a lead because of the potential danger to animals and other wildlife. Signs at the property will advise whether this is necessary.

No dogs. A few properties do not allow dogs at all.

Baby-changing and feeding facilities. This symbol indicates that there are facilities for baby changing and feeding, often in a purpose-designed parent and baby room.

Front-carrying baby slings for loan. Baby back-carriers cannot usually be admitted to houses because of the danger of accidental damage. This symbol indicates whether front slings are available for loan as a substitute. Babies carried in front slings are obviously very welcome.

Arlington Court

Historic house Carriage collection Garden Park Farm Lake Wood

Most people bring back a few things when they go on holiday abroad, but one-time owner Rosalie Chichester just didn't know when to stop – the house is packed with fascinating objects!

Animal antics
Rosalie's three peacocks, Spangles, Sapphire and Speckles, were allowed to wander about inside the house. The ponies and sheep you'll see are descendants of animals she introduced to the estate.

What to see
- Cabinets full of model ships, seashells, silver spoons and stuffed birds.
- In the nursery, a clockwork tortoise and a Victorian trapeze artist in a glass case (that's a model, not stuffed).
- Over 50 horse-drawn carriages – and one designed to be pulled by a dog.

What to do
- Grab the reins and 'drive' the 'please touch' carriage – the metal horse won't go far, though. Take a carriage ride in the 12-hectare (30-acre) grounds. Take a peek at the Bat-Cam – see bats roosting in the roof (May–Aug).

Special events
Look out for our 'Experience Carriage Driving Day', take the reins yourself in our two horse-power vehicle. There are also events for younger members of the family at other times, so get in touch.

By the way...
- There's a children's play area, baby-changing facilities and you can borrow a child sling. Children's menu in the Old Kitchen Tea-room.
- For those with mobility problems, there are many steps to the entrance, so ask us about the alternative entrance (near the tea-rooms). We have wheelchairs to book.

Arlington, nr Barnstaple,
Devon, EX31 4LP
01271 850296

OPENING TIMES

House
18 Mar–28 Oct 11am–5pm,
Mon–Fri, Sun

Carriage Collection
18 Mar–28 Oct
10:30am–4:30pm, Mon–Fri,
Sun

Gardens, Bat-Cam
18 Mar–29 Jun 10:30am–5pm
Mon–Fri, Sun
1 Jul–31 Aug 10:30am–5pm
Mon–Sun 1 Sep–28 Oct
10:30am–5pm Mon–Fri, Sun

Shop/tea-room
As gardens
2 Nov–16 Dec 11am–4pm
Fri–Sun

Notes
Whole property open Sats of BH weekends; other Sats in Jul & Aug only gardens, bat-cam, shop & tea-room open. Carriage rides available most days, tel. to check. Light refreshments only 3 Nov–17 Dec. Grounds open dawn–dusk 1 Nov–Mar 2007

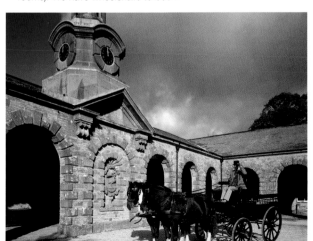

Avebury
Countryside Museum

Nr Marlborough,
Wiltshire, SN8 1RF
01672 539250

OPENING TIMES

Stone circle
All year Mon–Sun

Museum/Galleries
1–31 Mar 10am–4pm Mon–Sun
1 Apr–31 Oct 10–6pm Mon–Sun
1 Nov–28 Feb 08 10–4pm
Mon–Sun

Circle restaurant
1–31 Mar 10am–3:30pm
Mon–Sun
1 Apr–31 Oct 10am–5:30pm
Mon–Sun
1 Nov–28 Feb 08 11am–3:30pm
Mon–Sun

Shop
1–31 Mar 11–3:30pm Mon–Sun
1 Apr–30 Sep 10–5pm Mon–Sun
1 Nov–28 Feb 08 11am–4pm
Mon–Sun

Notes
Parking rebate gives receipt
holder free access to museum,
Alexander Keillier Museum (Barn
Gallery & Stables Gallery). EH
members free. Stone circle free

Avebury's prehistoric stone circle is one of the biggest in Europe and is thought to date back over 6,000 years. Voted the third most spiritual place in England, it is considered a Sacred Site and is still a shrine for Druids across the UK who gather here during the Summer Solstice. Ranking alongside the Taj Mahal and the Pyramids as one of the 440 World Heritage Sites, it is not to be missed. Soak up the special ambiance of this ancient sacred space, then discover more! See Life in Neolithic Times, Interactive Displays and Fascinating Finds in the Museum galleries!

Megalithic mystery
For centuries it was thought many of the missing stones had been demolished or stolen, but the technological magic of geophysics recently discovered at least 15 more, buried in the ground. It's thought they may have been pushed over and hidden in the 13th or 14th centuries, when people thought they were dangerous pagan symbols.

What to see
- The massive standing stones, arranged in circles.
- The Barber Surgeon's Stone – where the remains of a medieval man with some scissors in his pocket were discovered in 1938.
- The huge ditch around the stones, dug by picks made from antlers, and shovels made from the shoulder blades of oxen.
- Archaeological finds and audio-visual displays that tell the story of the stones.

What to do
- Discover more about 'Marmalade Millionnaire' Alexander Keiller's megalithic discovery. One of his great passions was archaeology – he used his fortune to buy and excavate the site at Avebury and re-erected many of the stones in the 1930s.
- The Stables Gallery depicts life in Neolithic times – there is even an example of Neolithic 'doggie do'. The Barn is home to 5 species of bats, the interactive 'Story of the Stones' and also a superb vintage car (a 1914 Sizare Berwick) that belonged to Alexander Keiller himself!

Special events
Including: Easter trails, 'Stones, Bones, Groans, Bats & Marmalade Trail', 'Time Travellers' Footprints Trail', 'Ugly Bugs & Lady Bugs Trail', plus 'Spooks & Spoofs' and 'Ghosts & Ghouls' Days. Living History Craft Workshops, Art Exhbitions and Special Interest Talks & Tours also offered.

By the way...
- Dogs are allowed, as long as they are on a lead.
- There's a picnic area by the barn as well as a restaurant.
- We have baby-changing facilities and there's no problem bringing your pushchair or baby-carrier.
- The museum is accessible, but only parts of the Circle are. There's a Braille and large print guide, as well as items that can be handled. Please book if possible.

Brownsea Island

Countryside Coastline Nature reserve Harbour

Brownsea Island is an unspoilt natural haven with a colourful history. It has been a coastguard station, a Victorian Pottery and even a daffodil farm, and was once the perfect haunt for smugglers who used to hide their booty in the castle. Now it's one of the last places where you can see red squirrels as well as many different kinds of seabirds. There are many walks on its 500 acres, some suitable for even the youngest would-be smuggler. Explore this relaxing car-free place, and admire the spectacular view across Poole harbour towards Studland and the Purbeck Hills.

Poole,
Dorset, BH13 7EE
01202 707744

OPENING TIMES

Island, Shop & Coffee Shop
24 Mar–20 Jul 10am–5pm
21 Jul–2 Sep 10am–6pm
3 Sep–29 Sep 10am–5pm
30 Sep–28 Oct 10am–4pm
Mon–Sun

Wartime disguises

During the Second World War, Brownsea Island was used as a decoy to protect the nearby towns of Poole and Bournemouth from Nazi bombing. Fires were lit on the island to confuse the pilots into thinking they had already reached their target. Today the many bomb craters on the island have become important habitats for rare wildlife.

What to see
- A variety of wildlife, including red squirrels and deer.
- Cormorants, oyster-catchers, terns, shelduck and other sea-birds, nose-diving into the sea.
- Proud peacocks strutting their stuff alongside free-ranging chickens.
- Excellent views from the cliffs, To the south-east you can see the chalk formations, Old Harry Rocks – supposedly where the devil laid down for a moment. (Old Harry's wife, a smaller rock, collapsed some time ago!)
- The stretch of water between Brownsea and Furzey, known as 'Blood Alley' because it is so shallow.
- A fascinating collection of restored 19th-century carts, wagons and machinery from Brownsea Island, near the Visitor Centre.

What to do
- Take the boat to Brownsea from Poole Quay and Sandbacks (every half-hour). Services available from Bournemouth and Swanage (See local information for fares and timetables).
- Follow the Smugglers' Trail to the treasure chest, with letter clues along the way. Ideal for 6-10 year-olds, it takes around an hour, with a Smuggler's certificate and sticker at the end. Or follow the Explorers' Trail, with simple map-reading required to find letters on posts. For a longer walk, take the Historical Trail round the island and a look at the ruins of the old pottery.
- Watch the birds on the lagoon from the public hide (designed with full wheelchair access).
- Take a picnic, or pick up a lunch box from the café.
- In the summer go for a guided walk in the nature reserve, which is not usually open to the public. Contact the Dorset Wildlife Trust warden on 01202 709445

Special events
There are many fun family events held throughout the year, including daily summer and half-term holiday activities like storytelling, pottery

continued…   17

demonstrations and special picnics or walks. The island is also home to the Brownsea Open Air Theatre, which puts on a Shakespeare play every summer.

By the way...

- If you have small kids, we can provide a free loan of one of our all-terrain baby buggies to help you get around. We also have a larger buggy for older children with restricted mobility. The rough terrain means that certain parts of the island are not very accessible, although there are tractor trailer trails for disabled visitors Mon-Fri (please contact to book).
- The castle isn't open to the public, and part of the island is a nature reserve with an additional charge. Sorry, no dogs allowed on the island because of the wildlife.
- There's a Coffee Shop near the landing quay, as well as a sweet shop that also sells ice cream and cold drinks.

Buckland Abbey

Historic house Garden Countryside

Set in a beautifully secluded valley, near the Tavy river, the ruins of the 13th-century abbey church point to Buckland's origins as a medieval monastery. Later the abbey was converted to a house by seafarer Sir Richard Grenville. But it's most famous as home to Grenville's arch-rival, Sir Francis Drake. In fact it's rumoured that Drake still haunts the 700-year-old building, along with his 'hell hounds'. There is much interesting memorabilia about him as well as interesting grounds to explore, including an Elizabethan garden.

Bowled over

The well-known story goes that Sir Francis Drake was enjoying a game of bowls in 1588 when news came that the Spanish Armada had sailed into view. Unperturbed, he carried on to finish his game, before going on to win the battle against the Spanish.

What to see

- The hand-crafted plasterwork ceiling in Drake's Chambers. A replacement for the original, which burnt down – believe it or not, this new one is made of yak hair plaster.
- The 'magic' drum in the Treasures Gallery. It's said that if ever England is in danger you should beat the drum and Drake will rise from the dead.
- The traditional craft workshops in the ox sheds, where you can see crafts like wood turning. The original monastery's chancel arch, still visible on the wall of the abbey's tower.

Yelverton,
Devon, PL20 6EY
01822 853607

OPENING TIMES

Estate/garden/restaurant/shop
1 Mar–11Mar 12:30pm–5pm Sat, Sun
17 Mar–28 Oct 12:30pm–5:30pm Mon–Wed, Fri–Sun
3 Nov–2 Dec 10:30am–5pm Sat, Sun
6 Dec–23 Dec 11am–5pm Thu–Sun

Abbey
1 Mar–11Mar 2pm–5pm Sat, Sun
17 Mar–28 Oct 10:30am–5:30pm Mon–Wed, Fri–Sun
3 Nov–2 Dec 2pm–5pm Sat, Sun
6 Dec–23 Dec 11am–5pm Thu–Sun

Notes
Winter admission (1 Nov–18 March): Reduced price for house; grounds free

continued…   19

What to do

- Discover how to find your way on the oceans with replica Tudor navigational instruments.
- Have a go at butter-making or old-fashioned tub laundry.
- Pick up a map at reception, and follow any of four woodland walks.

Special events

There are many special events suitable for all. Regular events include an Elizabethan Weekend, with dancing workshops, live music and cooking in the Kitchen. Also a recreation of a Medieval encampment, complete with craft demonstrations. There are often children's activity days with games, puzzles and hands-on activities. Get in touch to find out what's on, as booking is sometimes necessary.

By the way...

- There is picnic space in the car park and also the quarry orchard.
- The normal visitor route has many steps, and the grounds are only partly accessible. Alternative routes and wheelchairs are available. There are Braille guides and touchable objects.
- Children should be accompanied by an adult for family events (and vice versa!)
- Dogs are welcome in the car park only, and only on leads. There are dog posts in the shade so your furry friend can wait in comfort.

Chedworth Roman Villa

Museum Roman villa

A stately home with a difference – it's over 1700 years old. Here are the remains of one of the largest Romano-British villas in the country, nestled in a beautiful wooded valley in the heart of the Cotswolds. Unlike some Roman sites, here a lot has been uncovered and you can really get a sense of how the villa would have been.

Hypo heat
Did you know that the Romans had fancy underfloor heating to keep their toes warm? You can still see evidence of hypocausts at Chedworth – that's special flooring that was held up by columns to let the hot air through.

What to see
- Mosaics, bath-houses, latrines (Roman loos).
- The remains of a water-shrine.
- About 1.6 kilometres (over a mile) of ancient walls.

What to do
- Follow the site trail and imagine life as a rather posh Roman. Our audio-visual show brings the archaeology to life.

Special events
There are archaeological events throughout the year, and we also have special holiday activities and weekend days – like recreations of life as a gladiator (including battles) and spooky Halloween days.

By the way...
- Most of the site has steps although the entrance is ramped and we have a wheelchair. We have lots of 'living history' events with re-enactors to talk to and artefacts to handle.

Yanworth, nr Cheltenham, Gloucestershire, GL54 3LJ
01242 890256

OPENING TIMES
3 Mar–1 Apr 11am–4pm
Tue–Sun
3 Apr–28 Oct 10am–5pm
Tue–Sun
30 Oct–11 Nov 10am–4pm
Tue–Sun

South West

Corfe Castle

Ruins   Visitor centre

The Square, Corfe Castle,
Wareham, Dorset, BH20 5EZ
01929 481294

OPENING TIMES

Castle
1 Mar–31 Mar 10am–5pm Daily
1 Apr–30 Sep 10am–6pm Daily
1 Oct–31 Oct 10am–5pm Daily
1 Nov–28 Feb 10am–4pm Daily

Shop
As for castle

Tea-room
1 Mar–31 Mar 10am–5pm Daily
1 Apr–30 Sep 10am–5:30pm
Daily
1 Oct–31 Oct 10am–5pm Daily
1 Nov–28 Feb 10am–4pm Daily
Closed 25, 26 Dec. Tea-room
closed two weeks in Jan 2006
for internal repair and
decoration, tel. for details

Notes
High winds may cause closure
of parts of grounds

A storybook ruined castle – the inspiration for Kirren Castle in Enid
Blyton's *Famous Five* books. Corfe Castle was built in the 11th
century by William the Conqueror and has a history full of violence
and murder. After years as an important stronghold, the castle was
destroyed by Parliamentarians in the later 1600s.

Wicked old John

In the 13th century King John went to great lengths to improve the
building. He built a fine hall and chapel, and buildings for his domestic
staff. But he also ordered twenty-two knights to be locked in the grisly
dungeons and starved to death – he wasn't exactly one for modern
prison methods.

What to see

- Spooky ruins and even some medieval loos.
- Murder holes in the gatehouse – soldiers would fling stones, boiling
  oil and other nasties through them at their enemies below.

What to do

- Pop in to the Visitor Centre to find out what Lady Bankes thought
  about those medieval loos, and which English king was the first to
  wear a dressing gown. And while you're there, play with all the
  interactive displays and exhibitions.
- Picnic in the tiny ruins of West Mill where, in Victorian times, three
  families lived.
- Follow the children's quiz and trail. Take a walk through the Purbeck
  countryside by following one of our self-guided trails.
- Walk down to the village, also called Corfe Castle, where it's thought
  football may have been invented.

Special events

Loads! Family Fun Days with treasure trails in the grounds and storytelling.
Open air cinema in the castle grounds. Children's theatre shows and lots
more. We have lots of free holiday activities for which you don't need to
book.

By the way...

- Find out if the Swanage Steam Railway is open when you plan your visit – they operate a steam train service to the nearby station.
- Baby-changing facilities, children's menu. Pushchairs and back-carriers are fine, children must be accompanied in the castle.
- Please keep Rover on a lead.
- There is a fragrant medieval herb garden, many touchable areas, and a magnetic 'build a castle' display in the Visitor Centre.
- Mostly accessible, some steep slopes.

Castle Drogo

Castle Garden Park Countryside

South West

Drewsteignton, nr Exeter,
Devon, EX6 6PB
01647 433306

OPENING TIMES

Castle
3 Mar–11 Mar 11am–4pm
Sat–Sun
17 Mar–28 Oct 11am–5pm
Mon, Wed–Sun
29 Oct–4 Nov 11am–4pm
Mon, Wed–Sun
1 Dec–23 Dec 12pm–4pm
Sat–Sun

**Garden, Shop, Visitor Centre
and Visitor tea-room**
3 Mar–11 Mar
10:30am–4:30pm Sat–Sun
17 Mar–28 Oct
10:30am–5:30pm daily
29 Oct–4 Nov
10:30am–4:30pm Daily
5 Nov–23 Dec 11am–4pm
Fri–Sun

Castle tea-room
31 Mar–28 Oct 12–5pm Mon,
Wed–Sun

Notes

Croquet lawn normally open
June–Sept; equipment hire from
visitor reception

Situated high on a rocky outcrop above the dramatic Teign Gorge, it looks like a real medieval castle but it's actually an early 20th-century confection designed by the famous architect Edwin Lutyens. Inside it's a modern, comfortable home with a large garden to let off steam in.

Supermarket man

The first owner, Julius Drewe, became a millionaire at age 33 through his chain of grocery shops. He really wanted to have famous ancestors so he 'discovered' that he was descended from a Norman baron called Drogo de Teign – hence the name of the castle! Spot the fake castle features like arrow slits and portcullis.

What to see

- Family events programme running from March to December, with trails, re-enactments, themed weekends and something to do daily during school holidays. See how many lions you can see – it was the family emblem. Look in the Bunty House in the garden, where Julius' grandchildren used to play and see if you can find the two Castle cats Boots and Fluffy.

What to do

- Walk down the servants' staircase – they had their own, so that the family wouldn't have to bump into them. Find the telephone and the lift, which were 'mod-cons' at the time. Have fun doing one of the three free family trails in the house and then claim your prize.

Special events

Easter Egg trail, family trail and activity every day of the school holidays, week of Halloween activities, woodland sculpture workshops, Drogo Christmas with Father Christmas.

By the way...

- There's a children's play area and we can lend you hip-carrying infant seats. Baby-changing facilites and picnic area.
- There's a children's quiz/trail and a family guide.
- Wheelchairs available and ramped entrance, but no access upstairs.

Dyrham Park

Historic house Garden Park

There's a welcoming atmosphere at Dyrham Park on a Sunday afternoon, with lots of relaxed families picnicking on the grass in front of the house. Search for the furry maple, and other oddly named trees, and head down to the fascinating 19th-century 'below stairs' rooms.

Double Dutch

Look out for all things Dutch in the house, such as blue-and-white Delft china and lots of tulips. The reason? The house was built c.1700 for William Blathwayt, Secretary at War to Dutchman, King William III.

What to see

- A clever trick painting by the Dutch artist Samuel van Hoogstraeten. It'll really confuse everyone!
- The fascinating Victorian 'below stairs' rooms. You'll get a good idea of how hard servants worked when you see the huge kitchen ranges and other equipment.
- Peacocks and fallow deer in the park and some wonderful sounding trees – the 'strangle tree', the 'lanky lime' and the 'furry maple'.

What to do

- Imagine you're Sarah Saunders, the housekeeper here in 1710. She wrote down every single item in the house for an inventory. What a task!
- Go for a park walk and hoard your precious findings in a paper bag.

Special events

Dyrham occasionally runs family events. Check for details.

By the way...

- Treat your kids to a children's book illustrated by Ben Blathwayt, a descendant of the first owner – it's on sale in the shop. Have a picnic at Old Lodge and play on the tractor.

Dyrham, nr Bath,
Gloucestershire SN14 8ER.
0117 937 2501

OPENING TIMES

House
17 Mar–28 Oct 12pm–5pm
Mon, Tue, Fri, Sat, Sun

Garden/shop/tea-room
1 Mar–16 Mar 11am–4pm
Sat–Sun
17 Mar–28 Oct 11am–5pm
Mon–Sun
3 Nov–1 Jan 08 11am–4pm
Sat–Sun

Plant sales
17 Mar–30 Sep As shop

Park
All year 11am–5pm Mon–Sun

Cornish Mines & Engines

Visitor centre Mine

South West

Pool, nr Redruth,
Cornwall, TR15 3NP
01209 315027

OPENING TIMES

Centre/shop
4 Apr–31 Oct 11am–5pm Mon,
Wed, Thu, Fri, Sun

Today Cornwall's landscape is dotted with disused mine shafts and engine houses, a dramatic reminder of the time when this part of England was the centre for tin, copper and china clay mining. This World Heritage Site gives you a chance to find out what it must have been like in the 19th century, when the great steam-powered beam engines were used for pumping water up from depths of over 500 metres (1640 feet), and for winding men up and down into the mines.

Knock knock, who's there?

Maybe working down below with tapping picks and shovels, by candlelight, brought on that feeling of being watched. Cornish legends abound with tales of pixies and sprites, including the 'knockers' – invisible elfin creatures who supposedly lived in the mines. Fearing bad luck if they upset these rather pesky spirits, miners would leave them a portion of their own meal before going on with their work.

What to see

- The massive 75-cm (30-inch) working beam engine, which extends up three floors of the mine building, with huge piston rods and wheels.
- The even larger 225-cm (90-inch) engine used to pump water from the mine's murky depths (not working now).

What to do

- Visit the Industrial Discovery Centre, which provides an overview of Cornwall's mining heritage, and has a fascinating film.
- Follow the children's quiz/trail to make the visit more fun for younger visitors, as well as going to many events held at the property.

By the way...

- There's a lift which takes disabled visitors up and down the engine house. The lower part of the Engine House is accessible by ramp.
- Many of the original artifacts are available to touch, and there are guides who will be happy to assist.
- Not open between November and March, except by arrangement.
- Nearby working Levant Mine & Beam Engine (Trewellard, Pendeen, nr St Just, Cornwall TR19 7SX, 01736 786156) is also NT-owned.

Dunster Castle

Castle Garden Park

This fantasy castle with its fairy-tale turrets and towers is largely a 19th-century recreation. Enjoy exploring the zig-zagging paths of the gardens and tiptoeing around the spooky crypt!

Tall tale

In the 1870s workmen found at 2.3-metre (7-foot) skeleton in what was known as an 'oubliette' – a tiny cell in which a prisoner was locked up and left to rot. No one knows the identity of the mysterious skeleton.

What to see

- It's worth cricking your neck to catch a glimpse of the intricate plasterwork in the ceiling of the dining room which dates from 1681.
- Watch out in some of Dunster Castle's rooms for spooks, as they are reputedly haunted by a man in military uniform, a lady in grey and a disembodied foot!

What to do

- Children can poke their heads into the secret compartment (probably a priest's hole) in King Charles's bedroom. It may have connected with an escape passage to the village. Elderly people have memories of playing in the passage as children.
- Take a picnic and sit under the stunning 300-year-old oak tree after wearing everyone out with activity sheets and quizzes.

Special events

Dunster hosts some great events, including Easter Egg trails, Civil War living history, Pirates' Days and Halloween fun. Contact the property for more details.

Dunster, nr Minehead,
Somerset, TA24 6SL
01643 821314

South West

OPENING TIMES

Castle
23 Mar–25 Jul 11am–4pm
Mon–Wed, Sat–Sun
27 Jul–2 Sep 11am–5pm
Mon–Wed, Sat–Sun
3 Sep–31 Oct 11am–4pm
Mon–Wed, Sat–Sun

Garden/Park
1 Mar–22 Mar 11am–4pm Daily
23 Mar–31 Oct 10am–5pm
Daily
1 Nov–31 Dec 11am–4pm Daily

Shop
23 Mar–25 Jul 10:30am–5pm
Daily
27 Jul–2 Sep 10:30am–5:30pm
Daily
3 Sep–31 Oct 10:30–5pm Daily
1 Nov–1 Jan 08 11am–4pm
Daily
5 Feb 0–29 Feb 08 11am–4pm
Daily

Notes
25% discount for visitors with W Somerset Railway ticket

Finch Foundry

Museum River

Sticklepath, Okehampton,
Devon, EX20 2NW
01837 840046

OPENING TIMES
17 Mar–28 Oct 11am–5pm
Mon, Wed–Sun

The Finch brothers set up this water-powered foundry in 1814 to make mining and agricultural tools. At one time 400 tools a day were sharpened here. Three waterwheels drove the huge tilt hammer and grindstone, which you can still see today.

It's a dog's life
Workers had to lie flat across the stone wheel to reach it with their tools for sharpening. In winter that was a rather chilly experience, so dogs were especially trained to sit on the men's legs to keep them warm!

What to see
- Three water wheels driving the huge tilt hammer and grinding stone (when working).
- An exhibition about all the different tools made here – from the Devon potato chopper to the swan neck hoe.

What to do
- Hourly demonstrations by volunteers and professional blacksmiths.
- The 'four village trail' walk that starts at the foundry.
- Explore the foundry building and garden.
- Try out the quiz and trail especially for younger members of the family.

Special events
Recent events have included an Industrial Archaeology Day, a tour of local industrial sites (transport provided) for would-be Time Team-ers. On or around Saint Clement's Day – the Blacksmiths' Saint's Day – we host a competition for blacksmiths from all over the country – not to be missed. Check with us to see what's on.

By the way...
- Dogs are welcome except in the tea-room and foundry during demonstrations.
- There's loads to touch, smell and hear – the crashing water, smell of the coke fire, metalwork objects.
- The shop has a level entrance but the foundry does have a few steps.

Glendurgan Garden

Garden Coastline Maze

This sheltered and warm sub-tropical garden was created in the 1820s, and developed by the Fox family over many years. It runs right down to the charming little village of Durgan and its sandy beach with a wealth of interesting rockpools. Everyone in the family will love the laurel maze, which looks like a serpent laid out on the grass and dates from 1833. There are also many rare and exotic plants, as well as carpets of wild flowers in the spring.

Shipping News

Alfred Fox, who started this wonderful garden, worked in the shipping industry. And his choice for the garden's location is no accident – nearby Fal estuary is a deep-water harbour that was the first port of call for ships coming back from the Americas, the Far East and Africa. Guess how the Fox family managed to import all those exotic plants and seeds!

What to see

- Giant rhubarb and the enormous tulip tree – called canoe wood by Native Americans, who could make a canoe out of a single trunk.
- If you're lucky, one of the rough-legged buzzards flying overhead.
- The reconstructed orginal cob and thatch schoolroom Holy Bank – a part of the garden planted with trees and plants mentioned in the Bible, including a yew, a tree of heaven and a crown of thorns.

What to do

- Get lost in the laurel maze, but don't panic – Mums and Dads (and older children) will be able to see over the 1-metre/3-foot high hedges.
- Swing on one of the six ropes around the enormous Giant's Stride – that's a maypole with attitude.
- Catch the ferry from Durgan beach to Helford village.

By the way...

- Only the garden is open to the public, the house is privately occupied.
- The grounds are not very accessible to disabled people due to steep paths, but the viewing path is, and so are the shop and café.

Mawnan Smith, nr Falmouth, Cornwall, TR11 5JZ
01326 250906

OPENING TIMES
1 Mar–27 Oct
10:30am–5:30pm Tue–Sat

South West

MILLS, MEN & MARVELLOUS MACHINES

How about a visit to an example of Britain's amazing industrial heritage? The National Trust cares for a broad range of industrial sites and buildings, together with the machinery inside them. They're a fascinating way to learn more about Britain's industrial past, and a real eye-opener for all members of the family. Often there's a chance to try things 'hands-on' and to see industrial machinery in action.

Quarry Bank Mill in Cheshire has working machinery, and a unique insight into the lives of pauper child workers. The **Wellbrook Beetling Mill** in Country Tyrone is another example of a textile mill, and still produces calico, which is for sale in the shop. Right in the middle of town the **Winchester City Mill** in Hampshire has hand-milling of flour, and you can often join in.

While we're talking water power, visit **Cragside**, the home of eccentric 19th-century inventor and engineer, William Armstrong. He used it to power his lifts, lighting and central heating, not to mention his loos! (Please phone for more details, as Cragside is being refurbished in 2007.) Then there's **Patterson's Spade Mill** in Templepatrick, Northern Ireland, the last surviving water-driven spade mill in Ireland – and still making spades today – and the **Finch Foundry** in Devon, where you can often see demonstrations of the machinery in action.

If you haven't got water power, then wind power's a fashionable choice! Just to show that there's nothing new under the sun, visit some of the many windmills in Britain at **Pitstone Windmill** in Buckinghamshire, **Bembridge Windmill** on the Isle of Wight or the wonderfully named **Horsey Windpump**, in Norfolk.

In fact the lists of mills, both water and wind-powered, is so long that we'll just list a few others here: **Houghton Mill** in Cambridgeshire, Nether Alderley Mill in Cheshire, **Stainsby Mill** in Derbyshire, **Bourne Mill** in Essex, and **Dunster Working Watermill** and **Stembridge Tower Mill** in Somerset. You can pretty much guarantee that where there's some windswept countryside or a rolling river, a mill was built to take advantage of all that free power!

Mining has always been a feature of Britain's past, and you can see powerful reminders at **Aberdulais Falls in Wales** – complete with water wheel and hydroelectrics – and the **Dolaucathi Gold Mines** in Carmarthenshire. Not much gold there now, but it's nice to dream! The **Cornish Mines and Engines** (awarded World Heritage Site status in 2006) are partly restored to working condition, and remind us of Cornwall's important mining history. You can see a giant 27-metre (90-foot) beam engine and visit a fascinating Industrial Discovery Centre to learn more. In Cumbria, the **Force Crag Mine** in Borrowdale was the last working mineral mine in the Lake District, and the buildings and machinery have been restored (it's very remote, so telephone to check when it's open!).

While no man is an island, so they say, Britain is. That means that coastal defences have always been important, since early times. The same building and mechanical innovations that brought mills and mining, also provided better military protection. On the Isle of Wight you can marvel at the original cannon at the **Needles Old Battery**, and explore the fascinating military history, or in East Anglia admire the Martello Tower at **Orford Ness**, built against a potential Napoleonic invasion. Orford Ness has a long military history through both World Wars, so if that's your interest you'll enjoy the many military buildings and exhibitions here. (Of course, fortifications and defences go back a long way to pre-industrial times – take a brisk Northumbrian walk along **Hadrian's Wall** and visit **Houstead's Fort** to see how the Romans did it).

Visit the National Trust website at **www.nationaltrust.org.uk** to find more information about the many other industrial and commercial buildings owned by the National Trust.

Killerton

Historic house Garden Park Countryside Museum Visitor centre

Broadclyst, Exeter,
Devon, EX5 3LE
01392 881345

OPENING TIMES

House and restaurant
14 Mar–31 Jul 11am–5pm
Mon, Wed–Sun
1 Aug–31 Aug 11am–5pm Daily
1 Sep–29 Sep 11am–5:30pm
Mon, Wed–Sun
1 Oct–31 Oct 11am–5pm
Wed–Sun
8 Dec–23 Dec 2pm–4pm Daily

Park and garden
Open all year 10:30am–7pm
Daily

Restaurant
As house 12pm–5pm

Tea room
1 Mar–31 Oct 11am–5:30pm
Daily
1 Nov–30 Nov 11am–4pm
Wed–Sun
1 Dec–24 Dec 11am–4pm Daily
6 Jan 08–24 Feb 08
11am–4pm Sat, Sun

House
14 Mar–31 Jul 11am–5pm
Mon, Wed–Sun

Notes

Garden and Park: reduced
rate Nov to Feb

Killerton was built in 1778 for the Acland family. After a fire in the 1920s the inside was redesigned, and it's now furnished in the style of a country house from between the two World Wars. The hillside garden is spectacular, and the huge park and woods encompass the two villages of Broadclyst and Budlake. Perhaps the most fascinating feature is the Paulise de Bush collection of costumes – over 9000 outfits.

Mind the dragon

Near Killerton House there's an old Iron Age hill fort known as Dolbury Hill. There's meant to be a lot of treasure buried in it that's guarded by the Killerton Dragon. Supposedly the dragon flies across the valley to the mound every night – we think that might be a bit of a shaggy dragon story...

What to see

- The Victorian laundry, with mangles and irons – no 'wash and wear' clothes then!
- The Bear House, a funny little summer house that was once home to a pet Canadian black bear.
- Lots of costumes from the 18th–20th century, all on display in the house.

What to do

- Try and find the ice house in the garden.
- Visit the Discovery Centre to try various activities (limited opening, check we're open before you come), and try the quiz and trail.
- Play with Victorian toys.

Special events

We have all sorts of special days, often on Sundays. Bat-watching evenings, autumn walks and a day when our portraits 'came to life' and talked about themselves were just a few recent ones. Booking is sometimes necessary, for evening events especially.

By the way...

- Doggy friends are only allowed in the park, on leads, but there is shady parking in the overflow car park.
- Lots of room to picnic in the park, and children's menus in both the restaurant and tea-room.
- A handling collection of touchable objects in the Discovery Centre.
- Quite a few steps to negotiate, but we can provide a ramp if you ask.

Lanhydrock

Historic house Garden Park Countryside

Lanhydrock is a magnificent Victorian country house, with servants' quarters, gardens and loads of period 'Upstairs/Downstairs' atmosphere. It is set in over 360 hectares (900 acres) of woods and parklands, and there are many different footpaths and trails. An earlier house burnt down in 1881, although a 17th-century wing with a 29m/32yd-long gallery remains. The present 19th-century building featured the latest in mod cons – central heating.

Picture this

Lanhydrock and its grounds starred in the film of *Twelfth Night* with Helena Bonham-Carter. It was dressed up a bit for the film – there was a temporary grotto built from sea scallop shells, and flowers, leaves and vines were strewn about inside to make it look dreamy and romantic. We've cleared up now!

What to see

- Look for mythical beasts and Old Testament characters in the Long Gallery ceiling.
- Lots of Victorian toys in the nursery.
- A moose head and a great big fishy pike.

What to do

- Visit over 50 rooms, packed with portraits, trophies and an authentic kitchen.
- Find out about our dormouse monitoring programme.
- Go mad in the adventure playground with wobbly bridge, scramble nets and animal sculptures.
- Pianists may play the piano in the Long Gallery.
- We have lots of family and holiday activities, including pond dipping,

Bodmin,
Cornwall, PL30 5AD
01208 265950

OPENING TIMES

House
17 Mar–30 Sep 11am–5:30 pm
Tue–Sun
1 Oct–31–Oct 11am–5pm
Tue–Sun

Garden
All year 10am–6pm Daily

Plant centre
1 Mar–31 Mar 11am–4pm Daily
1 Apr–30 Sep 11am–5:30pm Daily
1 Oct–31 Oct 11am–5pm Daily

Shop and refreshments
1 Mar–16 Mar 11am–4pm Daily
17 Mar–30 Sep 11am–5:30pm Daily
1 Oct–31 Oct 11am–5pm
Mon–Sun
1 Nov–24 Dec 11am–4pm Daily
5 Jan 08–15 Feb 08 11am–4pm
Sat, Sun

continued…

kite making and tractor rides and other events. Get in touch to find out when they're on.

Special events
Easter Egg Trails, Children's holiday activities, Estate Walks, Hallowe'en and Christmas family events, Summer Family Fun Day.

By the way...
- In spring, tiptoe through the bluebell woods. Pick up a leaflet on walks in the grounds.
- There are some stairs, but we have wheelchairs and alternative routes.
- It's quite a walk from the car park to the house, though we have a drop-off place.

Lydford Gorge

Countryside River Waterfall

Butterflies, darting dragonflies and damselflies, bugs and beetles and other mini beasts hiding under the fallen trees and logs that they call home. Watch out for the dipper bobbing by the river, and other woodland birds. Check out the 'what to look for' board at the entrance. You can't miss the thunderous White Lady Waterfall, which cascades 30 metres (90 feet) and not hear the thundering Devil's Cauldron.

Into the ravine

During the 17th century Lydford Gorge was infamous for being the hide-out of a large family of outlaws, the Gubbins, who terrorised the neighbourhood and stole sheep from the farms of Dartmoor. In the 19th century, when wealthy people couldn't go on the 'Grand Tour' of Europe because of the Napoleonic War, Lydford proved a good substitute tourist adventure, and has been an attraction ever since.

What to see

- Variety of wildlife: from glamorous butterflies, dragonflies and dazzling damselflies to creepy bugs and beetles hiding under the fallen trees and logs.
- Watch out for woodland birds, including the dipper bobbing by the river.
- Check out the 'what to look for' board at the entrance. You can't miss the thunderous White Lady Waterfall, which cascades 30 metres. And you'll definitely hear the thundering Devil's Cauldron.

What to do

- Short circular walks to the Waterfall and Cauldron or a 4.8-km (3-mile) circular walk of the whole gorge. Walk out over the bubbling Devil's Cauldron. Watch the wildlife.

Special events

There's a lot going on at Lydford for all the family. Past events include sculpture-making days, autumnal woodland walks, Fungi Forays and special storytelling and spooky trails for children, with some very spooky items hidden along the way. Some events are free with admission.

By the way...

- The walking is quite arduous, so it's not ideal for anyone with a heart complaint or other health issues, or for very young children. Dogs are welcome, if kept on a lead. Get more information on the walks from Visitor Reception at either entrance. There's a small shop, tearoom and a good picnic spot at the waterfall entrance.

The Stables, Lydford Gorge, Lydford, nr Okehampton, Devon, EX20 4BH
01822 820320

South West

OPENING TIMES
1 Mar–23 Mar 11am–3:30pm Fri– Sun
24 Mar–30 Sep 10 am–5pm Mon–Sun
1 Oct–28 Oct 10am–4pm Mon–Sun
3 Nov–30 Dec 11am–3:30pm Sat, Sun
15 Feb 08–29 Feb 08 11am–3:30pm Fri–Sun

Overbeck's

Historic house Garden Coastline Museum

South West

Sharpitor, Salcombe,
Devon, TQ8 8LW
01548 842893

OPENING TIMES
18 Mar–15 Jul 11am–5pm
Mon–Fri, Sun
16 Jul–2 Sep 11am–5pm Daily
3 Sep–30 Sep 11am–5pm
Mon–Fri, Sun
1 Oct–28 Oct 11am–5pm Mon–
Thur, Sun

Tea-room
As house, 11:30am–4:15pm

Visit this elegant Edwardian house and gardens to see the weird and wonderful artifacts collected by scientist and inventor Otto Overbeck, a real-life Nutty Professor. While you're there, explore the 3 hectares (7 acres) of beautiful exotic gardens and admire the stunning view over the Salcombe estuary. Or join the kids in following tracker packs and trails. The staff are friendly, and so is Fred the ghost, who you might find if you look carefully.

Don't try this one at home

One of Otto's more ambitious inventions was 'the popular rejuvenator'. It was meant to make people look young again by giving them an electric shock. You can check it out in the Staircase Hall. But we don't recommend you plug it in, however much you'd like to recapture your youth!

What to see

- Shark's teeth, a crocodile skull, bird's eggs and even hyena. droppings in Overbeck's strange natural history collection.
- Ship-building tools and model boats, including one of the *Phoenix*, built at Salcombe in 1836.
- Dolls, dolls' houses and tin soldiers.
- Real orange trees in the conservatory, and a Japanese banana plant in the exotic gardens.

What to do

- Follow the secret clues to the secret children's room crammed with old toys.
- Go on a ghost hunt for Fred the friendly ghost. There's a chocolate version in the shop, plus summer and Halloween ghost story events.
- Ask to hear the polyphon – a gigantic old-fashioned musical jukebox (a bit bigger than an iPod).
- Explore the garden with all your senses on a newly developed sensory trail.

Special events

Watch out for special events celebrating 60 years of Overbeck's being open to the public.

By the way...

- A wheelchair is available, but only the ground floor is accessible. The shop and restaurant have level entrances, and most of the grounds are accessible with assistance.

Saltram

Historic house Garden Park

Saltram stands high above the River Plym in a rolling and wooded landscaped park. With its magnificent white exterior and grand design you could be forgiven for thinking it's the biggest wedding cake in the world. Inside it's full of opulent plasterwork and interiors designed by Robert Adams in the late 18th century.

Sensible choice
Saltram was the film location for *Sense and Sensibility*. You may recognize it as Norland Park, the Dashwoods' home, in the film starring Emma Thompson, Kate Winslet and Hugh Grant, not to mention the dashing Alan Rickman. Sadly, they've all gone now.

What to see
- Fancy ceilings and even fancier Chinese wallpapers.
- Peek at the paintings – including some rather good ones by Sir Joshua Reynolds.
- An Orangery, and several strange little buildings in the garden.

What to do
- Imagine sitting down with the Dashwoods (or with Alan or Kate...) in that swanky dining room.
- Explore the good cycle paths and walks in the parkland.
- Visit the Art Gallery, selling local arts and crafts.

Special events
Easter Trails, craft fairs, summer school holiday activities, Halloween events.

By the way...
- Baby-changing facilities, children's play area, children's menu in the licensed restaurant. Wheelchairs can be booked.

Plympton, Plymouth,
Devon, PL7 1UH
01752 333500

South West

OPENING TIMES

Park
All year Dawn–dusk Daily

House
28 Mar–28 Oct 12pm–4:30pm
Mon–Thur, Sat, Sun

Garden
1 Mar–28 Oct 11am–4:30pm
Mon–Thur, Sat, Sun
29 Oct–28 Feb 08 11am–4pm
Mon–Thur, Sat, Sun

Gallery
1 Mar–27 Mar 11am–4pm
Mon–Thur, Sat, Sun
28 Mar–28 Oct 11am–4:30pm
Mon–Thur, Sat, Sun
29 Oct–23 Dec 11am–4pm
Mon–Thur, Sat, Sun

Shop
1 Mar–27 Mar 11am–4pm
Mon–Thur, Sat–Sun
28 Mar–28 Oct 11am–5pm
Mon –Thur, Sat–Sun

St Michael's Mount

Castle Garden Coastline

Marazion, nr Penzance,
Cornwall, TR17 0EF
01736 710507

OPENING TIMES

Castle/shop/restaurant
1 Apr–31 Oct 10:30am–5:30pm
Mon–Fri, Sun

Last admission
4:45pm on the island. Sufficient
time should be allowed for
travel from the mainland. Nov to
end March: open when tides
and weather favourable.

What could be more mysterious and romantic than a medieval
church and castle perched on a rocky island? At low tide you can
walk over the historic causeway, or you can take a boat trip when
the tide is up. The oldest buildings date from the 12th-century
Benedictine priory, and the more recent castle is still lived in by the
Aubyn Family who acquired the island after the Civil War.

Now that's sleep-walking

Legend has it that the mount was built by the Giant Cormoran, who
had a nasty habit of stealing people's sheep for his tea. Jack, a local
lad, decided to catch him out. He dug a big hole in the path from the
castle, then blew on his horn to wake Cormoran up. The sleepy giant
stumbled right into the pit.

What to see

- Interesting rooms from many different eras, and lots of winding
  corridors and nooks and crannies.
- The door to the dungeon – in the church where they found a
  skeleton 2.3 metres (7 feet) tall – maybe it's sleepy old Cormoran.

What to do

- Make a wish on the wishing stone by the church steps.
- Clamber up the cobbled paths – some are quite steep, so wear
  your walking shoes.
- Garden Trail. Try the quiz book (best for older children).

Special events

Music events and concerts.

By the way...

- Baby-changing facilities and children's menu in the Sail Loft
  Restaurant.
- Please note: the site is steep in parts and with cobbled and uneven
  surfaces.

Trelissick Garden

Garden Park Countryside Coastline River Beach

These famous gardens are very special, with tranquil terraces and glorious views. Wander in this peaceful, colourful environment, then pop into the shop, buy a plant or two, and have a sit-down at the restaurant.

Plants with attitude

All kinds of exotic plants here, including skunk cabbage (now, guess why!), Australian tree ferns (no, they don't wear cork hats) and lichen-covered logs. Of course, we have lots of nice blossoms too.

What to see

- A babbling brook weaving through the watercress beds in Namphillow Wood.
- Tiny escape ladders for hedgehogs by the cattle grids!
- Many river birds – look out for cormorants sunning themselves to dry their wings.

What to do

- Find the Celtic Cross summerhouse – a priest would preach to the fishermen here (do you think they stopped fishing?).
- Picnic on the lawns across the bridge from the Dell – it's a lovely spot.
- Work out the time from the sundial in the scented garden. You need to know your Roman numerals!

Feock, nr Truro,
Cornwall, TR3 6QL
01872 862090

OPENING TIMES
1 Mar–28 Oct
10:30am–5:30pm Daily
29 Oct–23 Dec 11am–4pm
Daily
27 Dec–31 Dec 11am–4pm
Wed–Sun
2 Jan 08–9 Feb 08 11am–4pm
Mon–Sun

Woodland walks
All year – Daily

continued…

39

Special events

We have family-friendly activities all year, including Easter egg hunts and theatrical events during the holidays. Call us to find out what's on.

By the way...

- The house isn't open to the public but there is a shop, art gallery, plant sales, restaurant and café – so quite a lot!
- Pushchairs and back-carriers are fine, and we have changing facilities.
- Pick up a woodland walk leaflet.

Ashridge Estate

Countryside Visitor centre

About 2025 hectares (5000 acres) of woodland and open countryside running along the Herts/Bucks borders in the Chiltern Hills. Take a stroll, or go for something longer – there are more than enough splendid walks to tire out even the most energetic legs. Why not bring a picnic, and scrunch around in the leaves in autumn? A great place for the whole family to get out and about in the fresh air.

Bridge over troubled water?
The Bridgewater Monument in the grounds (near the Visitor Centre) was built in memory of the 3rd Duke of Bridgewater, better known as the Canal Duke. He built the United Kingdom's first canals to get coal from his mines to Manchester – although some say he actually built his canal to take his mind off a recent romance with the Duchess of Hamilton! From the top of the Monument on a clear day, you can see as far as London and Canary Wharf.

What to see
- Plenty of flora and fauna including fallow and muntjac deer and, if you're very lucky, badgers and woodpeckers. Bluebells carpet the area in spring and fallen leaves do the same in autumn.

What to do
- For a small fee, climb up the Bridgewater Monument (only 170 steps – what do you mean, 'my legs ache!'). Go for a nature walk, self-guided walks available from the shop, these include one for Ivinghoe Beacon by way of Steps Hill for a great view of the Chilterns.

Special events
Please contact us for details of our full programme of events for every age and interest.

By the way...
- We have a wheelchair available and maps of accessible routes on the Estate, as well as a number of PMV vehicles. Booking advisable.
- The shop and visitor centre are fully accessible.

Visitor Centre, Moneybury Hill, Ringshall, Berkhamsted, Hertfordshire, HP4 1LX
01442 851227

OPENING TIMES

Estate
All year Daily

Visitor centre/shop
17 Mar–16 Dec 12–5pm Daily

Monument
17 Mar–28 Oct 12–5pm
Sat, Sun

Tea-room
1 Mar–16 Dec 10am–5pm
Mon–Sun
1 Jan 08–29 Feb 08
10am–5pm Tue–Sun

Notes
Open BH Mons and Good Fri 12pm–5pm. Monument also Mon–Fri by arrangement, weather permitting. Shop closes at dusk if earlier than 5pm

Bateman's

Historic house Mill Garden

Burwash, Etchingham,
East Sussex, TN19 7DS
01435 882302

OPENING TIMES

House
17 Mar–28 Oct 11am–5pm
Mon–Wed, Sat, Sun

Garden/tea-room/shop
3 Mar–11 Mar 11am–4pm
Sat, Sun
17 Mar–28 Oct 11am–5pm
Mon–Wed, Sat, Sun
31 Oct–22 Dec 11am–4pm
Wed–Sun

Notes
Free entry to garden in Nov &
Dec

Did you like the film *The Jungle Book*? You'll be interested in this Jacobean house, home of Rudyard Kipling, who wrote the book it's based on. It's been arranged just as it was when he left, with his pen in the ink well awaiting new stories. Even his 1928 Rolls-Royce Phantom is outside waiting to rev up.

Why Why?
Kipling's elder daughter was called 'Elsie Why?' by the family because she was always asking questions. Do you know anyone like that?!

What to see
- The original illustrations for *The Jungle Book*.
- Oriental rugs and artifacts, brought home by Kipling.
- Find the sundial in the garden.

What to do
- Visit the water-mill, which generated electricity for the whole house. And we grind corn there most Wednesdays and Saturdays, at 2pm.
- Walk round the pond designed by Kipling to be shallow so that children could fall in safely (don't try it!).
- Hunt out the Kipling family initials, carved into the porch one rainy afternoon.

Special events

Recently we have had folk music in the garden, a Craft Fair and painting for children, with the cost usually included in the admission price.

By the way...

- We have a dog crèche where you can leave the pooch, and a picnic area near the car park.
- You can book a wheelchair, but there are some steps.
- There are many interesting objects in the house that you can touch (please ask).

43

Bodiam Castle

Castle Countryside Moat

South & South East

Bodiam, nr Robertsbridge,
East Sussex, TN32 5UA
01580 830436

OPENING TIMES

Castle
1 Mar–31 Oct 10:30am–6pm
Daily
3 Nov–17 Feb 08
10:30am–4pm
Sat, Sun
18 Feb 08–28 Feb 08
10:30am–6pm Daily

Shop, Tea-room
1 Mar–31 Oct 10:30am–5pm
Daily
1 Nov–23 Dec 10:30am–4pm
Wed–Sun
29 Dec–17 Feb 08
10:30am–4pm
Sat, Sun
18 Feb 08–28 Feb 08
10:30am–5pm Daily

A real 14th-century castle – with turrets, moat and all – situated by the River Rother in East Sussex. There are medieval battlements and ramparts galore, and spiral staircases to explore. One of the most famous and atmospheric places in Britain, Bodiam will leave a lasting impression on all the family.

My other house is a... castle

In 1385 Sir Edward Dalyngrygge was given permission to fortify his house against the invasion of France. But he decided to build a castle near his house instead. That's some extension...

What to see

- Four cylindrical towers at each corner, and four rectangular ones in between.
- Murder holes in the roof of the gatehouse, from which people dropped boiling water on the unsuspecting enemy.
- A Second World War pill box – where more recent soldiers lay in wait.

What to do

- Climb the towers, Walk the battlements and look out for enemy soldiers. Imagine living in the castle or staying in one of the guest rooms. Explore the nooks and crannies around the ruins. On particular days children can try on replica armour (tel. for details). Tracker packs and activity sheets are available for children.

Special events

We often have family and children's activities, including medieval weekends. Steam trains run on The Kent & East Sussex Railway right up to Bodiam, in season (not NT).

By the way...

- Dogs in the grounds are fine, but please keep your best friend on a lead.
- Pushchairs are admitted, and we have baby-changing facilities.
- Special menus in the tea-room, including dairy-free.
- Stairs to upper floors, and the grounds can be muddy.

Box Hill

Countryside Nature reserve Information centre

The Old Fort, Box Hill Road,
Box Hill, Tadworth,
Surrey, KT20 7LB
01306 885502

OPENING TIMES
All year Daily
Servery
25 Mar–31Oct 9am–5pm
Mon–Sun

1 Nov–29 Feb 08 10am–4pm
Mon–Sun
Shop/info centre
25 Mar–31Oct 11am–5pm
Mon– Sun

1 Nov–29 Feb 08 11am–4pm
Mon–Sun

Notes
Countryside free

You can't beat flying a kite up here on a billowy day, with gorgeous views over the South Downs and tons of fresh air. Bring a picnic and let the dog off the lead (except where there are sheep), and admire this outstanding area of woodland and chalk downland. Hop up to the top for a peek at a fort dating from the 1890s.

Boxed in?

Box Hill got its name from the box tree, which has grown here since at least the 16th century. Unfortunately it does pong a bit if you sniff it – some say it's a bit like tomcats. On a more savoury note – it was here that Jane Austen set the ill-fated picnic in her novel *Emma*.

What to see

- Tons of wildlife, including butterflies, tawny owls and kestrels. Look for the tracks of badgers and foxes, and you might see some if you're lucky.
- See if you can spot tiny bee orchids or wild strawberry plants in June and July.
- Visit our info centre at the summit and see natural exhibits like a badger's skull or a birds' nest.

What to do

- Stretch your legs walking through beautiful woods, or kicking a ball around.
- Or scrunch around in autumn leaves later on in the year.

Special events

A host of outdoor events take place every year at Box Hill. Ring the number above to find out details.

By the way...

- South scarp is very steep. If you have mobility problems, try the accessible paths along the North Downs Way.
- The Servery in the East car park has snacks and drinks, but isn't a full restaurant.
- We have baby-changing facilities; pushchairs are fine here, too.

Claremont Landscape Garden

Garden Lake Amphitheatre

These elegant gardens were begun in around 1715 and there are so many interesting features to explore in its 20 hectares (50 acres). There's a lovely serpentine lake, and island with a pavilion on it, a grotto, and an amphitheatre in the grass.

Gardeners' world
Some of the country's greatest gardeners had a say in designing Claremont – Sir John Vanbrugh, Charles Bridgeman and 'Capability' Brown, to name a few – fortunately not all at the same time.

What to see
- Lots of ducks near the lake – conveniently close to the car park.
- The grass amphitheatre – a kind of outdoor auditorium. Try sitting down up at the top and getting someone to talk at you from the bottom.
- Open air concerts are held here in summer; tel. for details.

What to do
- Have a picnic, or grab a cuppa in the tea-room.
- Go for a ramble – there are children's trails – and the lake one is suitable for buggies.

By the way...
- Dogs need to be on a lead, and can visit only between November and the end of March at the moment. There are some steep slopes but we have an accessible route. There are baby-changing facilities, and pushchairs are fine too.

Portsmouth Road, Esher, Surrey, KT10 9JG
01372 467806

OPENING TIMES

Garden
1 Mar–31 Mar 10am–5pm
Tue–Fri
1 Apr–31 Oct 10am–6pm Daily
1 Nov–28 Feb 08 10am–5pm
Tue–Sun

Shop/tea-room
1 Mar–31 Mar 10am–5pm
Tue–Sun
1 Apr–17 Dec 11am–5pm
Wed–Sun
13 Jan 08–28 Feb 08
11am–5pm
Fri–Sun

Notes
£1 tea-room voucher given if arriving by public transport (please present valid ticket) or cycle. No coaches on Sun or Bank Hols.

47

Dapdune Wharf & River Wey

Countryside River Old barge

South & South East

Navigations Office and
Dapdune Wharf, Wharf Road,
Guildford, Surrey, GU1 4RR
01483 561389

OPENING TIMES

Wharf
25 Mar–29 Oct 11am–5pm
Mon, Thur–Sun

Notes
(NB the shop and tea-rooms
are volunteer-run, not NT)
River trips 11am–5pm
(conditions permitting). Access
to towpath during daylight
hours all year

Back in 1653 the Wey was one of the first rivers to be made navigable and today, with its narrowboats and well-maintained towpath, it's a great place for a family adventure. You can clamber aboard *Reliance*, a restored barge, at Dapdune Wharf in Guildford, and boat trips are also available. If you'd rather stay on solid ground, there are some lovely walks on the tow path with friendly pubs nearby.

Beats the train?
The Wey Navigation linked Guildford to Weybridge and is over 19 miles long. Back in those days, getting goods from A to B involved large commercial barges pulled by horses from the towpath.

What to see
- The inside of the big old barge, *Reliance*.
- Lots of wildlife on the towpath, including kingfishers and roe deer.
- Don't miss our award-winning Visitor Centre.

What to do
- Guide a model barge through the lock in our interactive model.
- Take a 40-minute river bus trip on the *Dapdune Belle* (extra charge).
- Go fishing – get a permit from the Environment Agency or one of the angling clubs.

Special events
Easter egg trails, special Thursday activity days in August, lots of guided walks, including bat walks.

By the way...
- Nearly everything is accessible, maybe with a bit of help from a friend.
- There's a little shop and tea-room at Dapdune Wharf, and some nice riverside picnic areas.
- Please keep your dog on a lead around the wharf.

Devil's Dyke
Countryside Nature reserve

On a fine day, shove a coin in the telescope and you can see breathtaking views for up to 32 kilometres (20 miles) over the South Downs. The Dyke is the largest chalkland combe in Britain, and a favourite with walkers, energetic children, kite-flyers and very happy dogs.

A devil of a story
Rumour has it that the dramatic valley cut into the chalk was dug by the Devil in an attempt to flood the churches. Trouble is, he only had until sunrise to do his dastardly deed. Halfway through, he spied a candle in a window and heard a cock crow – fooled into thinking dawn had arrived, he scarpered without finishing the job.

What to see
- Look up at dare-devil hang-gliders floating through the sky.
- Look down to spot exotic orchids and nice-smelling herbs in the grass.
- Look out for information panels explaining the great views.

What to do
- Pedal your bike along the bridlepaths.
- Follow one of the self-guided walking tours – pick up our 'Delve into the Dyke' leaflet.
- Take the hugely popular route 77 bus from Brighton Pier to the Dyke (or back).

Special events
We have activities like Ugly Bug or Orchid Safaris and Devil's Dyke Detectives, and you can also go on one of our working holidays; get in touch to see what's on.

By the way...
- There's a very family-friendly pub by the car park, with great grub.
- There's a classic open-top bus service on Sundays and Bank holidays – pick up our 'Breeze up to the Dyke' leaflet.
- There are car parks right there, and an information trailer during the season.

West Sussex Downs Property Office, The Coach House, Slindon Estate Yard, Slindon, Arundel, West Sussex BN18 0RE
01243 814554

OPENING TIMES
All year

South & South East

COUNTRYSIDE CAPERS

Devon and Cornwall have some amazing stretches of coastal countryside. For family-friendly woodland strolls, try **Heddon Valley** with stepping stones and bridges along the river, or **Plym Bridge Woods**, which is great for walks and cycle rides. Not forgetting **Dartmoor National Park**, with great walking in **Whiddon Deer Park** and **Fingle Bridge**.

The East of England has both open countryside and some fascinating historical sites. **The Whipsnade Tree Cathedral** in Bedfordshire is unique, or take a walk on the **Dunstable Downs, Wicken Fen** or in the extensive **Hatfield Forest**. In Hertfordshire there are miles of footpaths in the **Ashridge Estate** and Suffolk's 'Constable Country' has lovely pathways to **Dedham Vale**.

If you're off to the East Midlands, the **Peak District National Park** is the place to wander – we own over 12 per cent of it. Especially beautiful parts are **Dovedale**, the Longshaw Estate and the stunning drive (or walk) through **Winnats Pass**. For the brave and hardy, take in the impressive views from **Kinder Scout** (not for youngsters).

Northern Ireland is famed worldwide for its outstanding natural beauty, from the coastal paths at the foot of Ulster's highest mountain, **Slieve Donard**, to the gorse-covered Sperrin Mountains in the North. Don't forget the extraordinary **Giant's Causeway**, with extensive walks along the North Antrim Cliffs.

You're really spoilt for choice in North West England, with the Lake District, Cumbria, Cheshire and Merseyside to pick from. Pop over to **Helsby Hill** or **Alderley Edge**, just a stone's throw from Liverpool and Manchester. Make a Lakeland holiday of it, and explore the dunes at **Sandscale Haws**. Or move inland to **Arnside Knott** and **Holme Park Fell**, both wonderfully unspoilt areas with a wide variety of wild flowers and butterflies.

In the Lake District, explore the lovely walks through ancient forests at **White Moss Common** or be stunned by the dramatic waterfall at **Aira Force** – with all that water round, it's good to know that there are loos (as well as a tea-room) there! Consider a dip in **Tarn Hows**, a gorgeous lake with a pushchair-friendly circular walk, or take a cruise across **Coniston Water**.

The South East, one of England's most densely populated areas, has quite a bit of open space. **The White Cliffs of Dover** need no introduction, but there's also **Box Hill, Leith Hill** and, back in Kent, 4.8 kilometres (3 miles) of the scenic **Royal Military Canal**. **The Witley Centre** is a fascinating place to find out more on the countryside and its management. Sussex offers walks over open downland at **Crowlink** and **Devil's Dyke**. Around the river Thames and the Solent, there are countryside finds like **Coombe Hill,** and the famous horse cut into the chalk escarpment at **White Horse Hill**, in Oxfordshire (while you're there, visit **Uffington Castle** and nearby **Dragon Hill** – no dragons, we're sorry to say!).

Wales has just oodles of mountain scenery and lush green valleys. How about the family-friendly beaches at **Broadhaven**, Porthdinllaen and Llanbedrog, or even a chance to see dolphins at **Mwnt**? Then there are lovely summer meadow walks at **Lanlay Meadows**, freshwater lily ponds at **Bosherton** and the **Dommelynllyn Estate**, with one of Wales's most impressive waterfalls, **Rhaedr Ddu**.

Dorset, the Cotswolds and Gloucestershire have **Melbury Down**, a rich chalkland with lovely views, and **Haresfield Beacon** and **Minchinhampton** and **Rodborough Commons.** All are worth a look! A highlight for families is **Leigh Woods** in Bristol, especially if you have a pushchair to deal with. **Dyrham Park** also offers family parkland walks.

In the Midlands there's **Carding Mill Valley** and the former railway walk at the **Leak & Manifold Valley Light Railway** (don't worry, there are no trains now!). While you're in the area, enjoy the family events at **Dudmaston, Attingham Park** and, in particular, **Shugborough**, a working historic farm that always has a lot going on.

Last, but certainly not least, Yorkshire and the North East have amazing stretches of moorland and some of the most dramatic coastline in Britain. Explore miles of beautiful beaches, or move inland to **Wallington** or **Cragside** (closed for refurbishment in 2006/7), both properties with extensive grounds and loads of interest for younger folks.

And that was just a few of them! Visit the National Trust website at **www.nationaltrust.org.uk** to find more information on all the other countryside areas that you can explore.

Hughenden Manor

Historic house Garden Park Countryside Wood

High Wycombe,
Buckinghamshire HP14 4LA.
01494 755573

OPENING TIMES
House/grounds
3 Mar–28 Oct 1pm–5pm
Wed–Sun
1 Dec–16 Dec 12pm–1pm Sat,
Sun

Garden
3 Mar–28 Oct 11am–5pm
Wed–Sun
1 Dec–16 Dec 11am–4pm Sat,
Sun

Park
All year Mon–Sun

Shop/restaurant
3 Mar–28 Oct 11am–5pm
Wed–Sun (see also below)

Shop
3 Nov–16 Dec 11am–4pm
Wed–Sun

Restaurant
3 Nov–16 Dec 11am–4pm Sat,
Sun

Hughenden Manor was the much-loved country home of 19th-century Conservative Prime Minister, Benjamin Disraeli. Enjoy the manor filled with his pictures, books and furniture, and then take the family for a walk in the gardens and surrounding park and woodland. Be warned – it is very hilly in places. There are often extra children's activities going on.

'We authors, ma'am'
Disraeli was a great favourite with Queen Victoria, unlike the Liberal Prime Minister, William Gladstone, whom she thought addressed her like a public meeting. Both Disraeli and the Queen had written books – he was a very successful novelist, while she published an account of her travels in Scotland.

What to see
- The secret servants' doors in the dining room (if you can find them).
- Disraeli's own books, all 4,000 of them! On the staircase wall is his 'gallery of friendship', with portraits of his many friends, including the Queen and his devoted wife, Mary Anne.
- A marble copy of Mary Anne's foot – the Queen started a craze for this when she had her children's feet sculpted.
- The German forest planted by the Disraelis.

What to do
- Use the fun children's guide to explore the house and garden.
- Try out the family story trail – there's a leaflet to guide you on this half-hour walk round the estate.
- Go to the church and see the monument put up by Queen Victoria to her favourite Prime Minister.
- Enjoy a scrumptious lunch or tea in the Stableyard Restaurant.

Special events
There are lots of great events at Hughenden. For details, please contact us. There will be a small charge for most events.

By the way...
- For £3 a day you can hire a super-tough, all-terrain buggy, to negotiate the bumpy ground on the estate walks.

Ightham Mote

Historic house Garden Countryside

Ightham Mote is a romantic moated medieval and Tudor manor house, built around a courtyard. It's so hidden away that even Cromwell's soldiers got lost trying to find it in the dark and looted a nearby house instead. The Mote started life in 1320 but has been added to by various owners, including the Selby family, who lived in it from the end of the Elizabethan period right through to Victorian times. Over the years it has acquired a painted Tudor ceiling, a Jacobean fireplace, Chinese 18th-century wallpaper and a 19th-century billiards room.

Remember remember...
The story goes that Dame Dorothy Selby sent a letter warning Lord Monteagle not to attend Parliament on 5th November 1605 – the night of the Gunpowder Plot. But her letter gave the game away, and supporters of Guy Fawkes were so angry that they locked her in a secret room in the house, and left her there to die. Years later, some workmen discovered some bones. Who knows if they are Dame Dorothy's, but perhaps if you notice a chill in the air, you'd better watch out – just to be on the safe side.

What to see
- Perhaps the only house with a Grade I-listed dog kennel, made in 1890 for Dido, a St Bernard dog who was so big her food had to be served in a washing-up bowl.
- All the owners had different building ideas and no building restrictions, so look out for several different types of chimney.
- There's a slit in the wall near the entrance gate, known as a parley hole. In medieval days people would post letters or speak through it to ask if they could come into the building.

Mote Road, Ivy Hatch, Sevenoaks, Kent, TN15 0NT
01732 810378

OPENING TIMES

House
4 Mar–28 Oct
10:30am–5:30pm
Mon, Wed–Fri, Sun

Garden
4 Mar–28 Oct 10am–5:30pm
Mon, Wed–Fri, Sun

Estate
Open daily all year, dawn to dusk

Restaurant/shop
4 Mar–28 Oct 10am–5:30pm
Thu–Sat
1 Nov–28 Oct 11am–3pm
Mon, Wed–Fri, Sun
1 Feb 08–24 Feb 08 11am–pm
Thu–Sat

South & South East

continued... 53

What to do

- Squint through the squint window in the Chapel. And what on earth is a putlog? Try and hug the massive sweet chestnut trees, which measure over 8 metres (23 feet) around. Explore the gardens, which provided the medieval house with food.

Special events

There are many different events during the season, and quite a few are suitable for all the family. Recent activities have included woodcarving and cookery demonstrations and special drawing workshops for children. Some children's activities involve a small additional fee. It's a good idea to phone first to see what's on, and booking is sometimes necessary.

By the way...

- Ightham Mote was the subject of the largest conservation project ever undertaken by the National Trust on a house of this kind, which started in 1988 and was only finished in 2004.
- Contact us in advance for information on the wide range of touchable objects.
- There are many scented plants in the garden.
- Wheelchairs are available, as well as portable ramps. Some of the grounds and upper floors of the house are not accessible easily.

The Needles Old Battery

Countryside Coastline Fort

This Victorian fort is perched on the tip of the Isle of Wight in a stunning position overlooking The Needles rocks. If you have an interest in guns, ships and military matters, there's a range of things to explore here.

Battered about a bit
Did you know that a Battery is simply a collection of guns and artillery? In 1903 the obsolete guns were thrown over the cliff. Tsk! Later on, early anti-aircraft guns were tried out here and there were even rocket tests in the 1950s and 1960s. Don't worry, nothing's loaded now.

What to see
- Cartoons by acclaimed comic-strip artist Geoff Campion, which explain what went on at the Old Battery.
- A list of all the ships that have been wrecked on The Needles.
- Original cannons on display.

What to do
- Climb down the narrow spiral staircase and go through the 55-metre (60-yard) tunnel to the searchlight for a view of the Needles Rocks.
- Experience life as a soldier with the new children's explorer pack 'A soldier's life'.

Special events
Though we don't have many events we have an exhibition, and you might want to visit the nearby Bembridge Windmill while you're here – you can climb right up to the top.

By the way...
- We're afraid this site is somewhat inaccessible if you have mobility problems. The paths are steep and can be uneven. But the ground floor is accessible.
- The walk up to the Old Battery is 1.6 kilometres (roughly 1 mile) – so be prepared for a bit of a hike.

West Highdown, Totland, Isle of Wight, PO39 0JH
01983 754772

OPENING TIMES
Battery, tea-room
25 Mar–30 Jun 10:30am–5pm Mon–Thur, Sat, Sun
1 Jul–31 Aug 10:30am–5pm Daily
1 Sep–28 Oct 10:30am–5pm Mon–Thur, Sat, Sun

Tea-room
13 Jan–18 Mar 07 11am–4.30pm, Sat, Sun
3 Nov–16 Dec 11am–3pm Sat, Sun
12 Jan–18 Mar 08 11am–3pm Sat, Sun

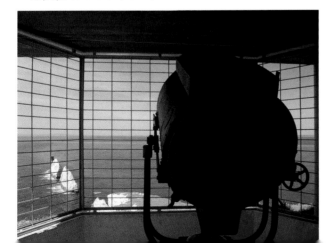

Petworth House & Park

Historic house Park Lake

Petworth,
West Sussex, GU28 0AE
01798 342207

OPENING TIMES

House
17 Mar–28 Mar 11am–4pm
Mon–Wed, Sat, Sun
31 Mar–31 Oct 11am–5pm
Mon–Wed, Sat, Sun

Shop/restaurant
10 Mar–28 Mar 11am–4pm
Mon–Wed, Sat, Sun
31 Mar–31 Oct 11am–5pm
Mon–Wed, Sat, Sun
7 Nov–24 Nov 10am–3.30pm
Wed–Sat

Christmas Shop
29 Nov–23 Dec 10am–3.30pm
Thu–Sun

Park
All year 8am–Dusk Daily

Pleasure ground/kitchens
10 Mar–28 Mar 11am–4pm
Mon–Wed, Sat, Sun
31 Mar–31 Oct 11am–6pm
Mon–Wed, Sat, Sun
7 Nov–24 Nov 10am–3:30pm
Wed–Sat
29 Nov–16 Dec 10am–3:30pm
Thu–Sun

A magnificent 17th-century house and grounds with landscaping by 'Capability' Brown and more than 1000 fallow deer – probably the largest herd in Britain. The house is full of treasures and has the National Trust's finest collection of paintings – including 19 paintings by Turner, who lived here for a while.

I do, I do, I do – but don't sit down!

Elizabeth Percy, who inherited Petworth in 1682, married three times before she was 16. Her third husband, the Duke of Somerset, was so full of his own importance that he cut one of their daughters out of his will because she dared to sit down while he was asleep! The same family has lived here for over 800 years and you can trace their family history through the many portraits.

What to see

- An original Victorian kitchen with copper pans, steamers and jelly moulds.
- See the giant trays which the footmen had to carry over to the dining room in the house.
- Look at the difference between the Servants' Quarters and the grand mansion.

What to do

- Walk in the park and look out for the famous Petworth herd of fallow deer and old trees.

- Follow the children's quiz through the house and use your detective skills – Tracker Packs are available for young children.

Special events
Packed programme of Family Events all season – get in touch with us for more information.

By the way...
- There are wheelchairs available, and a ramped entrance. Baby changing facilities are available and there is a children's menu in the restaurant.

Polesden Lacey

Historic house Garden Park

Great Bookham, nr Dorking,
Surrey, RH5 6BD
01372 452048

OPENING TIMES
House
17 Mar–28 Oct 11am–5pm
Wed–Sun

Garden/shop/tea-room
1 Mar–28 Oct 11am–5pm Daily
29 Oct–23 Dec 11am–4pm
Daily
3 Jan–28 Feb 08 11am–4pm
Daily

Notes
Croquet lawns and equipment
for hire from house (book in
advance).

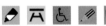

Step back into the 1920s, stroll through the house and grounds and imagine you're a house guest of the Hon Mrs Greville, a society hostess who lived here. In 1923 the future King George VI and Queen Elizabeth spent some of their honeymoon in this elegant Regency villa, and must have enjoyed its opulent interiors and beautiful rose garden.

Party party...
Mrs Greville threw many lavish parties for the rich and famous and entertained all kinds of royalty. She came from quite humble origins as the daughter of William McEwan – founder of the brewery. This was just her country home – she had another one for her London parties.

What to see
- Lady G's mementoes from her parties, kept in a special book – you can even find out what her guests had to eat.
- Gleaming gilt-covered walls and a chandelier with nearly 4000 pieces that takes over a week to clean.
- Lovely gardens – find Lady Greville's gravestone in the rose garden.

What to do
- Croquet anyone? Have a go on the croquet lawn, you can hire equipment from us (please book in advance).
- Test your brains with the house quiz.
- Run around in the children's play area and try the adventure trail.

Special events
There are often events in the grounds, including sheepdog trials and vintage car rallies. We have Fungus Forays and other nature walks, as well as a summer festival and children's events.

By the way...
- There are wheelchairs available, and a ramped entrance. There are steps to the upper floors and elsewhere.
- Call first and we'll arrange touchable objects for you to try.
- Baby-changing, children's menu and hip-carrying child slings available.

Sheffield Park Garden

Garden Countryside Lake

This lovely 'Capability' Brown garden is nowhere near Sheffield. Sheffield means 'sheep clearing', and the park is actually recorded first in the Domesday book. The 49 hectares (120 acres) of garden have trees and shrubs from all over the world. Be a family of plant hunters as you explore the garden together!

Lady of the lake

According to legend there's a lady ghost between the third and fourth lakes, known as Upper and Lower Woman's Way Pond. You could wave, but she wouldn't see you – apparently she has no head!

What to see

- In spring there are tons of daffodils and bluebells, with a rainbow of colour in May.
- Autumn is pretty fantastic too as the garden shows off its wonderful leafy colours.
- Don't miss the waterfall, cascades and four large lakes (and the odd duck – well, more than one odd duck!).

What to do

- Explore the garden with one of our family Tracker Packs or be an artist for the day with the Artist's Pack.
- The Bluebell Steam Railway is just up the road, and there's a joint ticket you can buy to combine it with your visit.

Special events

Family events throughout the year, including Teddy Bears' Picnic and family fun days – please call for details.

By the way...

- Baby-changing facilities. Pushchairs and back-carriers are fine, and we can loan you an all-terrain pushchair or back-carrier.
- No pets, it's just not suitable.
- Four wheelchairs available and a map of an accessible route. Some of the grounds have steep slopes.

Sheffield Park,
East Sussex, TN22 3QX
01825 790231

OPENING TIMES

Garden/shop
1 Mar–29 Apr
10:30am–5:30pm Tue–Sun
1 May–3 Jun 10.30am–5:30pm Daily
5 Jun–30 Sep
10:30am–5:30pm
Tue–Sun
1 Oct–4 Nov 10:30am–5:30pm Daily
6 Nov–23 Dec 10:30am–4pm
Tue–Sun
27 Dec–30 Jan 10:30am–4pm
Wed–Sun
5 Jan 08–28 Feb
10:30am–4pm Sat, Sun

Notes
Joint ticket with Bluebell Railway available. RHS members free.

Witley & Milford Commons

Heaths   Woodland   Visitor centre

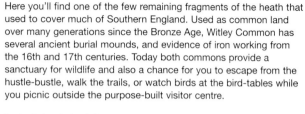

Witley Centre,Witley,
Godalming, Surrey, GU8 5QA
01428 683207

OPENING TIMES
Centre
25 Mar–29 Oct 11am–5pm
Sat, Sun, 11am–4pm Tue–Fri
Common
Open all year, daily.

Here you'll find one of the few remaining fragments of the heath that used to cover much of Southern England. Used as common land over many generations since the Bronze Age, Witley Common has several ancient burial mounds, and evidence of iron working from the 16th and 17th centuries. Today both commons provide a sanctuary for wildlife and also a chance for you to escape from the hustle-bustle, walk the trails, or watch birds at the bird-tables while you picnic outside the purpose-built visitor centre.

Left right, left right
During the First and Second World Wars, the commons were used as a training camp for the army. There were up to 20,000 soldiers marching around on it at one time. A Polish contingent of soldiers planted Hawthorn around their barracks, to cheer things up a bit. In the late 1940s, the parade ground was broken up, and the land was restored to its pre-war condition. Now the commons are a Site of Special Scientific Interest.

What to see
- The Green Hairstreak and Silver-Studded Blue. No, they're not punks, they're butterflies!
- Woodpeckers and nuthatches on Witley Common.
- Dartford warblers and nightingales on Milford Common.
- See if you can spot lizards, adders (watch out!) and roe deer.

What to do
- Bring a picnic and relax.
- Pick up a quiz sheet from the Witley Centre and go on one of the nature trails over heathland and woodland.
- Visit the countryside exhibition and try out the special puzzles and quizzes for the younger members of the family.
- Have a cup of tea and watch the wildlife.

Special events
Get in touch to find out what events we have on. Past activities have included Pond Dipping for bugs and creepy crawlies, and a Night Hike for bats. Booking is essential, and children must bring an adult along too.

By the way...
- The grounds are partly accessible, but it can be a bit muddy in wet weather. There are two wheelchairs available at the Witley Centre, as well as an adapted WC. The shop and picnic tables are accessible.
- There's a touch table of objects you can handle, and a guide in braille.

Ham House

Ham House is unique in Europe as the most complete survival of 17th-century fashion and power. One of a series of palaces and grand houses along the banks of the Thames, it was built in 1610 and enlarged in the 1670s, when it was at the heart of Restoration court life and intrigue.

Spooky stories

Ham House was home to the extravagant Duchess of Lauderdale, who was renowned as a political schemer during the Civil War and Restoration period. She is said to still haunt its passageways. In fact, there are so many phantom tales of Ham, that it is reported to be one of the most haunted houses in England.

What to see

- The lavish 17th-century interiors with a wealth of textiles, furniture and paintings.
- Visit the service buildings. See the earliest identified Still House in England and the dairy with cast iron 'cow's legs'.

Ham Street, Ham,
Richmond-upon-Thames
TW10 7RS
0208 9401950

OPENING TIMES

House
31 Mar–28 Oct 1pm–5pm Mon, Tue, Wed, Sat, Sun

Garden
All year 11am–6pm Mon, Tue, Wed, Sat, Sun

Shop/café
1 Mar–18 Mar 11am–4pm Sat, Sun
24 Mar–28 Oct 11am–5:30pm Mon, Tue, Wed, Sat, Sun
3 Nov–16 Dec 11am–4pm Sat, Sun (see also below)

Café
6 Jan 08–29 Feb 08
11am–4pm Sat, Sun

Shop
1 Mar 08–29 Feb 08
11am–4pm Sat, Sun

Notes
Admission to garden includes outhouses and introductory video

London & East

continued… 61

What to do

- After-dark 'Ghost' tours for Halloween and daytime family Ghost tours during school holidays. Booking essential.
- Christmas family events include carol concerts and special 'below-stairs' openings when the kitchen and other servants' areas will be dressed in a Christmas theme from times gone by.
- Family tracker packs throughout the open season both in the house and the garden.

Special events

Easter trails, theatre in the garden and special Christmas openings. Please check the Ham House section on the website for updates. Alternatively contact the property for an events leaflet.

Morden Hall Park

Garden Park Countryside Farm Nature reserve Visitor centre Waterways

It's not often you can find a huge park so near a London Underground station. And Morden Hall's parkland is not your average back garden, with over 50 hectares (125 acres) of rose garden, meadows and wetlands to explore. A river runs through it – follow its meanders and bridges and you'll come to the two water mills, used until 1922 to grind snuff. You can still see the original waterwheel that turned the millstones to crush the tobacco. Morden Hall itself, built in 1770 and owned by Westminster Abbey, is now a popular restaurant.

The park was home to the local philanthropist Gilliat Hatfeild. He is well remembered and loved by local people for his many acts of kindness, including holding tea parties for local school children before the war. Mr Hatfeild was a great lover of trees and open spaces and, like his father, he shunned the 20th century. The family built stables to travel by horse and carriage, and their passion for fishing is even seen in the weather vanes on top of several buildings.

What to see
- Coots, moorhens, mallard ducks and herons on the waterways.
- All kinds of fish in the Capital Garden Centre's aquaria.
- Outside the mill, two of the millstones that used to grind the tobacco.

What to do
- Play games in open parkland, wander by and across the River Wandle (a variety of bridges).
- Have a picnic in the fenced dog-free paddock especially for families.
- Visit the independently run Deen City Farm (at the northern edge of the park), where you can stroke rabbits and guinea pigs, and see baby goats, Jacob sheep and Derek, the snow-white peacock. Usually open Tuesday–Sunday.
- In season, smell the roses – there are over 2000 of them so that's quite a sniff – or should that be snuff...

Special events
A programme of family events is run in the Snuff Mill. Holiday activities every Thursday in school holidays and discovery days one Sunday a month. Please ring us to find out more.

By the way...
- The park is ideal for family cycling because it's flat, and the Wandle Trail passes right through it.
- Well-behaved dogs will enjoy a run in the parkland, but must be kept on leads near buildings and in the rose garden.
- The shop and café are accessible, but some of the paths in the park are not. There is recently improved access to the Snuff Mill, as well as an adapted WC.
- Braille and large print guides, and interesting things to hear and smell.

Morden Hall Road, Morden, London, SM4 5JD
020 8545 6850

OPENING TIMES
Park
All year 8am–6pm Mon–Sun

Shop
All year 10am–5pm Mon–Sun

Café
All year 10am–5pm Mon–Sun

London & East

63

Osterley Park & House

Historic house Garden Park Lake

Jersey Road, Isleworth,
London, TW7 4RB
020 8232 5050

OPENING TIMES

House/Jersey Galleries
14 Mar–28 Oct 1pm–4:30pm
Wed, Thu, Fri, Sat, Sun
1 Dec–16 Dec
12:30pm–3:30pm Sat, Sun

Shop
14 Mar–28 Oct 12:30–5pm
Wed, Thu, Fri, Sat, Sun
31 Oct–16 Dec 12–4pm Wed,
Thu, Fri, Sat, Sun

Tea-room
1 Mar–2 Mar 12–3pm Sun
3 Mar–11 Mar 11:30am–5pm
Sat, Sun
14 Mar–28 Oct 11:30am–5pm
Wed, Thu, Fri, Sat, Sun
31 Oct–16 Dec 12–4pm Wed,
Thu, Fri, Sat, Sun

Park
30 Oct–24 Mar 8am–6pm
Mon–Sun
25 Mar–28 Oct 8am–7:30pm
Mon–Sun
All year 8am–6pm Mon–Sun

House/Jersey Galleries
14 Mar–28 Oct 1pm–4:30pm
Wed, Thu, Fri, Sat, Sun

Osterley is a beautiful house and park within easy reach of central London. It is a great place to escape the city and you might see rabbits, squirrels, ducks and even parakeets. Originally a Tudor house, it was transformed in the 18th century into its present elegant appearance.

Heartbreak house

In 1782, Sarah-Anne Child, the 18-year-old daughter of Osterley's owner, ran away to Gretna Green to marry the Earl of Westmoreland. Soon afterwards her father died, some say of a broken heart.

What to see

- In the park you can see 400-year-old oak trees and lots of other rare and exotic trees.
- In the spring there are lots of bluebells and in summer time, Mrs Child's Flower Garden is full of flowers.
- In the house, look for marigolds in the decorations on the walls and furniture. The marigold was the emblem of the Child family who used to live here.

What to do

- Borrow our family Tracker Packs for either the house or park and discover more about Osterley with lots of fun activities for you to do.

Special events
There are family events throughout the year. The highlight of the summer is the annual Osterley Day which takes place in July. This is a community and arts event, with something for the whole family to enjoy. Other past events include Easter trails, fun days and tours of parts of the house not normally open to visitors, including the roof.

By the way...
- Baby slings and hip-seats can be borrowed in the house; pushchairs are admitted when visitor numbers allow.
- There are baby-changing facilities available.
- Children's menu and high chairs available in the tea-room.

Sutton House

Historic house

2 & 4 Homerton High Street,
Hackney, London, E9 6JQ
020 8986 2264

OPENING TIMES
Historic rooms
1 Mar–23 Dec 12:30pm–4:30pm
Thu, Fri, Sat, Sun
Art gallery/shop/café-bar
1 Mar–23 Dec 12pm–4:30pm
Thu, Fri, Sat, Suns

Here's an unexpected gem of a Tudor house, hidden right in the middle of East London. It's well worth a visit to explore its atmospheric interior, enjoy the peaceful courtyard and grab a bite to eat at the cosy café.

Hackney house
Difficult to believe that Hackney was once a pretty village outside London, but it was in 1535 when the house was built! Sutton House has been a rich merchant's home, a school, and a place of recreation for poor working men. Now it's a venue for concerts and art exhibitions.

What to see
- Fine Tudor oak panelling and carved fireplaces.
- Doors and panels that open to reveal parts of the original house – including two 'garderobe' loos – no longer in use!
- Paintings and artwork by local artists.

What to do
- Creep around in the old cellars.
- Explore the exhibition that tells the story of the house.
- Touch (and smell!) objects in the authentic Tudor kitchen.

Special events
We have many events, including monthly Family Days full of fun activities. Come on a ghost tour (if you dare!) or enjoy children's activities at our Craft Fair.

By the way...
- There's a children's quiz/trail and baby-changing facilities.
- We have a wheelchair – you need to book it – but there are stairs to upper floors.
- Worth checking that we're open to the public before you visit – there are sometimes special private events.

Belton House

Historic house Garden Park

This magnificent country house was built in 1685–89 for 'Young' Sir John Brownlow, and it's thought that the architect of St Paul's Cathedral, Sir Christopher Wren, had a hand in its H-shaped design. There are fine paintings and carvings inside, and 14 hectares (36 acres) of gardens, with a beautiful Lakeside Walk.

Belting around Belton

Belton was the film location for the BBC's *Pride and Prejudice* as well as the children's serial *Moondial* and their recent production of *Jane Eyre*. And you can act, too – there's Victorian clothing for all the family to try on. Take it off to play in our other attraction – the National Trust's largest adventure playground.

What to see

- Look out for all the animals used in the decorations and paintings in the house.
- Look up to see some very ornate ceilings.
- Look down to find a fancy painted floor in one of the rooms.

Grantham,
Lincolnshire, NG32 2LS
01476 566116

OPENING TIMES

House
17 Mar–28 Oct 12:30pm–5pm
Wed, Thu, Fri, Sat, Sun

Garden/park
17 Mar–31 Jul 11am–5:30pm
Wed, Thu, Fri, Sat, Sun
1 Aug–31 Aug
10:30am–5:30pm Mon–Sun
1 Sep–28 Oct 11am–5:30pm
Wed, Thu, Fri, Sat, Sun
2 Nov–16 Dec 12pm–4pm Fri,
Sat, Sun
3 Feb 08–25 Feb 08
12pm–4pm Sat, Sun

Adventure playground
17 Mar–31 Jul 11am–5:30pm
Wed, Thu, Fri, Sat, Sun
1 Aug–31 Aug
10:30am–5:30pm Mon–Sun
1 Sep–28 Oct 11am–5:30pm
Wed, Thu, Fri, Sat, Sun

Shop/restaurant
17 Mar–31 Jul 11am–5pm
Wed, Thu, Fri, Sat, Sun
1 Aug–31 Aug 11am–5pm
Mon–Sun

Notes
'Hidden England' passport scheme: with a stamped passport, one person can obtain free admission when a full-price ticket is purchased from other properties in the 'Hidden England' group

continued…   67

What to do
- Visit the activity room upstairs to try on costumes or come along to the Belton Discovery centre.
- Swing, climb and slide away around the mega-sized adventure playground – the less energetic can watch from the picnic area!
- Trails available for the house and gardens.

Special events
Get in touch to see dates for our next family days. We often have special walks, or even a chance to try your hand at crafts or archery.

By the way...
- Grab a family guide or activity pack to help you explore.
- Very baby-friendly, with facilities, and carriers to borrow.
- Wheelchairs available but there are many steps up to the entrance. Map of accessible route in grounds.

Blickling Hall, Garden & Park

Historic house Garden Park Countryside Lake

Blickling Hall is a quirky-looking building and has a sumptuous collection of Dutch gables and turrets, striking brick chimneys and some massive yew hedges. The present building was built in the early 17th century and is one of England's great Jacobean houses, with a spectacular Long Gallery, and fine collections of pictures, books and tapestries. Wander in its extensive gardens and parklands, with something to see throughout the year and lots of interesting walks to explore.

Heads or tales

Henry VIII's second queen, poor old Anne Boleyn, lived in an earlier house at Blickling when she was young. Bet she later wished she'd stayed at home instead of marrying Henry, who had her beheaded. Some swear they've seen her headless ghost riding up to the house, in a coach pulled by headless horses.

What to see

- Anne Boleyn's life-size statue on the stairs (with head!).
- Some very curious beasts hiding in the plaster ceiling in the Long Gallery.
- A secret garden with a sundial.
- A pyramid. Well, not a real Egyptian one but a tomb – or mausoleum – built for one of Blickling's owners.

What to do

- Explore the park by following one of three waymarked walks. Pet dogs can come too if kept on a lead.
- Have a picnic in the orchard, or by the visitor reception area.
- See if you can spot local wildlife, including woodpeckers, herons and owls.

Blickling, Norwich,
Norfolk, NR11 6NF
01263 738030

OPENING TIMES

House
17 Mar–22 Jul 1pm–5pm Wed, Thu, Fri, Sat, Sun
23 Jul–2 Sep 1pm–5pm Mon, Wed, Thu, Fri, Sat, Sun
5 Sep–28 Oct 1pm–5pm Wed, Thu, Fri, Sat, Sun

Garden
17 Mar–22 Jul 10:15am–5:15pm Wed, Thu, Fri, Sat, Sun
23 Jul–2 Sep 10:15am–5:15pm Mon, Wed, Thu, Fri, Sat, Sun
5 Sep–28 Oct
10:15am–5:15pm Wed, Thu, Fri, Sat, Sun
1 Nov–29 Feb 08 11am–4pm Thu, Fri, Sat, Sun

Park
All year Dawn–dusk Mon–Sun

Plant centre
17 Mar–28 Oct
10:15am–5:15pm Wed, Thu, Fri, Sat, Sun

Shop
As garden

Restaurant
As garden

House
17 Mar–22 Jul 1pm–5pm Wed, Thu, Fri, Sat, Sun

Note
Free access to South Front, shop, restaurant, plant centre, secondhand bookshop, art exhibitions. Coarse fishing in lake; permits available at lakeside

continued…   69

Special events

Family-friendly activities include sculpture workshops, open-air theatre and giant garden games. Get in touch to book.

By the way...

- At the weekends and during school holidays you can hire bicycles to explore the park.
- The basement rooms are not accessible except by stairs, but the rest of the house is, and we have wheelchairs available. The garden and other facilities are fully accessible, with maps of special routes.
- We have braille and large print guides, and a handling collection.

Dunstable Downs

Countryside Visitor centre Whipsnade Estate

The Downs are a large area of chalk grassland and farmland that's a haven for wildlife. A great place to stretch your legs and get lots of fresh air. It's the highest spot in Bedfordshire and has wonderful views out over the Vale of Aylesbury and along the Chiltern Ridge. The Icknield Way is possibly the oldest road in England.

Downs in disguise
During World War II the Meteorological Office at Dunstable was camouflaged to look like part of the Downs. The buildings and tennis court were covered with leaves and nets, and one of the buildings was disguised as a haystack!

What to see
- Flying of all kinds – planes on their way to Luton airport, gliders, paragliders and kites.
- Or put your nose to the ground to look for interesting plants and creatures.

What to do
- A very popular kite-flying spot. If you don't have one, we sell a large range in the shop.
- Pop into the popular Chilterns Gateway Centre, a very family friendly place.
- Bring your bike – it's OK to cycle on the bridleway.

By the way...
- The centre is fully accessible and a popular family place.

Dunstable Road, Whipsnade, Bedfordshire
LU6 2TA. 01582 608489

OPENING TIMES

Downs
Open all year Daily

Shop
25 Mar–29 Oct 10:30am–5pm Mon–Fri
25 Mar–29 Oct 10–5pm Sat
25 Mar–29 Oct 10–6pm Sun
30 Oct–18 Mar 07 10–4pm Sat, Sun

Kiosk
Open all year 10–dusk Daily

Note
Open BH and Good Fri.
Countryside Centre Call for opening times. Kiosk closed 25 Dec

Dunwich Heath & Beach

Coastal centre Countryside Coastline Nature reserve Visitor centre

Dunwich, Saxmundham,
Suffolk, IP17 3DJ
01728 648505

OPENING TIMES
7 Mar–15 Jul Daylight Wed,
Thu, Fri, Sat, Sun
28 May–3 Jun Mon–Sun
16 Jul–16 Sep Mon–Sun
19 Sep–21 Oct Wed, Thu, Fri,
Sat, Sun
22 Oct–28 Oct Mon–Sun
31 Oct–23 Dec Wed, Thu, Fri,
Sat, Sun
27 Dec–2 Jan 08 Wed, Thu, Fri,
Sat, Sun
5 Jan 08–24 Feb 08 Sat, Sun
13 Feb 08–17 Feb 08 Wed,
Thu, Fri, Sat, Sun

Notes
Car park charge for non-members

Dunwich Heath is a remote and beautiful place with a unique atmosphere. There are stunning views out over the sea and mysterious heathland walks over the gorse and heather, shady woods and crumbling sandy cliffs. It's a lovely place to walk, and then come back for tea at the old coastguard cottages.

A village in the sea
Perched high on the cliff, fronting the wind, are the white-painted Coastguard Cottages. Replacing an older, wooden structure, which was lost to the sea, the cottages were built in 1827 and for 80 years were home to frequently-changing families of coastguards charged with clearing the coast of smugglers. When the Admiralty finished with the buildings, the cottages became home to holidaymakers.

What to see
- The heathland at Dunwich supports the largest population of Dartford warblers in East Anglia along with other heathland specialists such as stonechat and meadow pipit, many solitary bees and wasps and butterflies such as the Greyling, Brown Argus and Green Hairstreak.
- The wetland along Dowcra's Ditch has fascinating dragonflies, damselflies and the rare ant-lion.
- The shingle banks on the beach support many wonderful plants such as yellow-horned poppy and during the summer the air is filled with the calls of sand martins which nest along the cliffs.

What to do
- Splash in the sea, or try a bit of beachcombing.
- Explore the heath and its rare wildlife.
- At the new Seawatch stations search for seals, porpoise or seabirds across Solebay.

Special events
Events leaflet available from March. Please get in touch.

By the way...
- We have holiday flats if you'd like to stay here longer.
- Heathland Explorers – our Children's Holiday Club – runs every Wednesday throughout the school holidays (April-October). Check for details.

Hatfield Forest

Countryside Nature reserve Lake Fishing

This ancient woodland is a rare surviving example of a Medieval Royal Hunting Forest. Today it is a paradise for walkers and families with young children. With 405 hectares (1000 acres) to explore, an exciting special events programme, a café selling homemade cakes and an 18th-century Shell House, there is something here for everyone. There are miles of grass tracks for cycling, cows roam freely in the summer months and signs of wildlife are apparent everywhere you go. This very special place is ideal for families to come and enjoy 365 days a year.

Ancient trees

Some of the trees in the Forest are over a 1000 years old, and the Doodle Oak in particular was metioned in the Domesday Book. There is evidence of an Iron Age settlement, and the deer that live in the Forest are thought to be descendants of the herds hunted by King Henry I.

What to see
- During summer, cattle grazing in the forest.
- Ducks and the occasional swan on the lake.
- The newly restored Shell House – open at weekends

What to do
- Get a day ticket to go fishing (July–Feb).
- Discover the forest by foot with a Trail Guide or by bike – there are several miles of grass paths available.

Special events

Trusty, the National Trust Hedgehog, sometimes comes along to give out stickers, and we have Halloween and Christmas trails. We have quite a few live music and craft events. Get in touch to see what's on ... full events list available.

By the way...
- Hatfield is both a National Nature Reserve and a Site of Special Scientific Interest.
- The visitor centre is fully accessible.
- Great place for picnics – but watch out for cowpats!

Takeley, nr Bishop's Stortford, Hertfordshire CM22 6NE.
01279 870678

OPENING TIMES
All Year Dawn–dusk Mon–Sun
Refreshments
1 Apr–31 Oct 10am–4:30pm Mon–Sun
4 Nov–29 Feb 08
10am–3:30pm Sat, Sun

Notes
Car park charge for non-members. Horse riding permits available via Hatfield Forest Riding Association, tel. for details

London & East

Houghton Mill

Mill

London & East

Houghton, nr Huntingdon,
Cambridgeshire, PE28 2AZ
01480 301494

OPENING TIMES

Mill/bookshop
24 Mar–29 Apr 11am–5pm Sat
24 Mar–29 Apr 1pm–5pm Sun
30 Apr–26 Sep 11am–5pm Sat
30 Apr–26 Sep 1pm–5pm Mon,
Tue, Wed, Sun
29 Sep–28 Oct 11am–5pm Sat
29 Sep–28 Oct 1pm–5pm Sun

Tea-room
As Mill 11am–5pm

Walks/car park
All year 9am–6pm Mon–Sun

Enjoy watching the wheels and cogs go round in this last working watermill on the Great Ouse, set on an island in the middle of the river. The impressive five-storey, 18th-century building has operational machinery, and you can see flour being produced before your eyes (and buy some to take home too). It's a lovely area to take a walk in, with riverside meadows and a trail around Houghton Village.

Watery power

Did you know that along with making flour, and pumping water, mills have also been used to produce paper and even gunpowder? The only milling that goes on at Houghton is of the floury variety although the water also drives a turbine that produces electricity for the building.

What to see
- All the water wheels, grinding stones, cogs and shafts – great if you're interested in how things work.
- Milling (on Sundays and Bank Holidays). Find out what a damsel or hopper was for.
- Look out on the nearby lock.

What to do
- Have a go at turning the model millstones and pulling on the rope to lift a bag of flour.
- Bike or horse-ride on the bridleway (but watch out if you're walking!).
- Stay in the nearby caravan and campsite (run by the Caravan Club).

By the way...
- The grounds are fully accessible, as is the ground floor of the mill. Phone ahead to make sure we're going to be milling if you want to see the wheel in action.

Ickworth House, Park & Gardens

Historic house Garden Park Wood

This very eccentric stately home, with a big central rotunda and curved corridors, was built in 1795 by an equally eccentric bloke, the 4th Earl of Bristol. Today you can see his fine Georgian silver, and paintings by Titian, Gainsborough and Velásquez. The fine 18th-century parkland is also worth exploring, with an Italianate garden, a vineyard, canal and lake.

Hervey going

Frederick August Hervey, aka the 4th Earl of Bristol, was Bishop of Derry for 35 years, but also enjoyed generally living it up. Lord Chesterfield said 'At the beginning God created three different species, men, women, and Herveys,' and Lord Charlemont added 'His genius is like a shallow stream, rapid, noisy, diverting, but useless'. With friends like that...

What to see

- The heraldic animal of the Hervey family, the snow leopard or ounce can be spotted (groan!) in almost every room in the house.
- An unusual collection of tree stumps and massive stones from the Giant's Causeway.
- Silver fish, fans, miniature paintings and lots of other objects.
- Outside, massive ancient oak trees in the park; spooky Gothic atmosphere of the Victorian Stumpery.

The Rotunda, Horringer,
Bury St Edmunds,
Suffolk, IP29 5QE
01284 735270

OPENING TIMES

House
17 Mar–30 Sep 1pm–5pm
Mon, Tue, Fri, Sat, Sun
1 Oct–4 Nov 1pm–4:30pm
Mon, Tue, Fri, Sat, Sun

Gardens
17 Mar–30 Sep 10am–5pm
Mon, Tue, Fri, Sat, Sun
1 Oct–29 Feb 08 11am–4pm
Mon, Tue, Fri, Sat, Sun

Park
All year 8am–8pm Mon–Sun

Shop/restaurant
17 Mar–4 Nov 10am–5pm
Mon, Tue, Fri, Sat, Sun
5 Nov–23 Dec 11am–4pm
Mon, Tue, Fri, Sat, Sun
27 Dec–1 Jan 08 11am–4pm
Mon, Wed, Thu, Fri, Sat, Sun
2 Jan 08–29 Feb 08
11am–4pm Mon, Tue, Fri, Sat, Sun

continued...   75

What to do

- Play in the adventure playground.
- Work out with the family on the woodland Trim Trail and Family Cycle Route (some steep terrain, helmets advised).
- Borrow a Park and Garden Activity backpack.

Special events

Guided walks in the woodland and secret garden, and lots of family activities ranging from Time Travelling to meeting Creepy Crawlies. Get in touch to see what's coming up.

By the way...

- 2007 is Ickworth's 50th Birthday. Contact us to see what special events for families are planned.
- Great new facilities for visitors are now open 12 months a year in the West Wing (including shop and restaurant).

Oxburgh Hall, Garden & Estate
Historic house Garden Wood Moat

You might see a swan float past your window in this grand manor house surrounded by a moat, and complete with battlements. The Bedingfeld family have lived here ever since the house was built in 1482.

Hidey-hole
After the Reformation, Catholic families like the Bedingfelds had a lot to fear, even death. The house has secret doors and a priest's hole, where they or their priest could hide if soldiers came.

What to see
- Look for the ha-ha – a ditch dug on the edge of a field to keep cows and sheep out. You can hardly see it, so don't fall in – ha ha!
- A huge Tudor gatehouse.
- The priest's hole – imagine how scary that would be.

What to do
- Take a peek at the little Catholic chapel in the grounds.
- Take the Woodland Explorer trail around the garden, or enjoy a picnic lunch in the car park.
- Check out where the drawbridge used to be.

Special events
We have family events like Easter egg hunts, and also Living History days when you can meet a variety of characters in Tudor costume. Check with us to see what's on.

By the way...
- There's a secondhand bookshop in the Gun Room, during season.
- Try out the children's quiz/trail and pick up information on self-guided family tours.
- Baby-changing facilities and children's menu.
- We have a ramped entrance and wheelchairs; there are stairs to other floors. And be careful near the moat!

Oxborough, King's Lynn, Norfolk, PE33 9PS
01366 328258

OPENING TIMES

Gatehouse
Limited guided tours of the Gatehouse showrooms at weekends 6 Jan–11 Mar 07 and 5 Jan–24 Feb 08

House
17 Mar–31 Jul 1pm–5pm Mon, Tue, Wed, Sat, Sun
1 Aug–31 Aug 1pm–5pm Mon–Sun
1 Sep–30 Sep 1pm–5pm Mon, Tue, Wed, Sat, Sun
1 Oct–28 Oct 1pm–4pm Mon, Tue, Wed, Sat, Sun

Garden/restaurant/shop
1 Mar–11 Mar 11am–4pm Sat, Sun
17 Mar–31 Jul 11am–5:30pm Mon, Tue, Wed, Sat, Sun
1 Aug–31 Aug 11am–5:30pm Mon–Sun
1 Sep–30 Sep 11am–5:30pm Mon, Tue, Wed, Sat, Sun
1 Oct–28 Oct 11am–4:30pm Mon, Tue, Wed, Sat, Sun

Sutton Hoo

Countryside Museum

Tranmer House, Sutton Hoo,
Woodbridge,
Suffolk, IP12 3DJ
01394 389700

OPENING TIMES
1 Mar–16 Mar 11am–4pm
Sat, Sun
17 Mar–1 Apr 11am–5pm
Wed, Thu, Fri, Sat, Sun
2 Apr–15 Apr 10:30am–5pm
Mon – Sun
16 Apr–27 May
10:30am–5pm Wed, Thu, Fri,
Sat, Sun
28 May–3 Jun 10:30am–5pm
Mon–Sun
4 Jun–1 Jul 10:30am–5pm
Wed, Thu, Fri, Sat, Sun
2 Jul–2 Sep 10:30am–5pm
Mon–Sun
3 Sep–21 Oct 11am–5pm
Wed, Thu, Fri, Sat, Sun
22 Oct–28 Oct 11am–5pm
Mon – Sun
29 Oct–26 Dec 11am–4pm
Sat, Sun
27 Dec–1 Jan 08 11am–4pm
Mon–Sun

Notes
Free entry for Education
Group members for booked
educational visits only.
Different admission prices, inc.
charge for NT members, on
certain special event days. Tel.

Sutton Hoo is one of Britain's most important and atmospheric
archeological sites. It was the burial ground of the Anglo-Saxon
kings of East Anglia. Visit the award-winning exhibition that explains
the burial mounds and tells the story of Anglo-Saxon warriors,
treasure and kings.

Underground treasure ship
In 1939 one of the large mounds at the site was excavated, revealing a
huge amount of priceless royal treasure inside the remains of a burial
chamber in a 27-metre (90-foot) ship. It's one of the most important
finds ever discovered in Britain, and is famous worldwide.

What to see
- Visit the viewing platform to see the large burial mounds, including
  the 'Treasure Mound'.
- A full-size reconstruction of the ship's burial chamber with copies of
  its treasures as they may have been.
- Find out how the exquisite jewellery was made.
- Displays change twice per year.

What to do
- Watch our specially commissioned film conjuring up the world of
  Anglo-Saxon kings, craftsmen and poets.
- Walk along the River Debden on waymarked trails – take binoculars
  if you can; there are lots of birds.
- Have fun in the children's play area, and try out the dressing-up box
  in the exhibition.

Special events
Our family events have included felt-making demonstrations, Easter
trail, Halloween Happenings (very spooky!) and crafts. Contact us to
find out what's planned.

By the way...
- Dressing-up box and quiz in exhibition.
- There are some tethering rings and water too, for doggy friends.
- Picnic area and children's playground.
- We have wheelchairs, and a map of an accessible route, the
  entrance is level.

Tattershall Castle

Castle

You can explore from the cellar to the battlements in this very dramatic medieval tower, with walls as thick as a room. It was built in the 1400s for Ralph, Lord Cromwell, a wealthy adviser to King Henry VI, and over one million locally made bricks were required to build the tower and buildings. There was an earlier fortified castle but this one was really made mostly for show.

It's a moat point
Well two, actually – the original castle on this site had an outer and inner moat, which have been restored. One 'for best' – for entertaining guests and visitors, so they say – and one to keep out nasty enemy gatecrashers.

What to see
- One vast tower – with four great chambers with enormous Gothic fireplaces and lots of tapestries.
- The very creepy cellar – go on, we dare you.

Tattershall, Lincoln,
Lincolnshire, LN4 4LR
01526 342543

OPENING TIMES
3 Mar–18 Mar 12pm–4pm Sat,
Sun
24 Mar–26 Sep 11am–5:30pm
Mon, Tue, Wed, Sat, Sun
29 Sep–31 Oct 11am–4pm
Mon, Tue, Wed, Sat, Sun
3 Nov–9 Dec 12pm–4pm Sat,
Sun

Notes
Free audio guide

continued… 79

What to do

- Dress up and play with Tudor toys and medieval costumes.
- Grab our free audio guide to find out more about 15th-century life.
- Walk over the moats (by way of the bridges, that is).

Special events

Fancy a spot of brass rubbing? On some Sundays we'll let you loose on our collection for a small charge. We also have children's activity days and living history weekends, get in touch.

By the way...

- We have some touchable objects and a braille guide too.
- There are stairs to the upper floors in the castle.

Wicken Fen

Mill Countryside Nature reserve Visitor centre Cottage

One of Britain's oldest nature reserves and a very special and ancient place. Once the whole of East Anglia was covered with fenland, which is a special kind of peaty wetland. Now this is the last 0.1% of natural fenland left. It's a haven for birds, plants, insects and all kinds of wildlife. Explore its lush green paths and visit the hides, or walk along the boardwalk (fine for pushchairs).

Not quite high and dry

Most of the fenland that was part of the Great Fen of East Anglia has now been drained and ploughed. That drainage made the level of the dry land fall, so that Wicken Fen is now left standing like an island, up to 2 metres (6½ feet) higher than the land around it.

What to see

- Butterflies, birds, bugs, reptiles, and rare plants like fen violet and milk parsley.
- Fen Cottage – a typical workers' dwelling built from products of the fen.

What to do

- Put on your wellies (it can be wet!) and take one of the trails – pick up a guide at the visitor centre.
- Bring your binoculars – or hire some from us – to look at the birds from Tower Hide.
- Have a very un-medieval ice cream after your walk!

Special events

We have quite a lot going on. Recently we have had bat and moth detection nights, ghosts' walks, wildlife identification and a chance to try your hand at rush weaving.

By the way...

- We have a couple of wheelchairs, and the boardwalk is accessible, as is the café and picnic area.

Lode Lane, Wicken, Ely, Cambridgeshire, CB7 5XP
01353 720274

OPENING TIMES

Reserve
All year Dawn–dusk Mon–Sun

Centre/shop
1 Mar–31 Mar 10am–5pm Tue, Wed, Thu, Fri, Sat, Sun
1 Apr–28 Oct 10am–5pm Mon–Sun
29 Oct–10 Feb 08 10am–4:30pm Tue, Wed, Thu, Fri, Sat, Sun
11 Feb 08–17 Feb 08 10am–5pm Mon –Sun
18 Feb 08–29 Feb 08 10am–5pm Tue, Wed, Thu, Fri, Sat, Sun

Café
1 Mar–31 Mar 10am–5pm Tue, Wed, Thu, Fri, Sat, Sun
1 Apr–28 Oct 10am–5pm Mon–Sun
29 Oct–10 Feb 08 10:30am–4:30pm Wed, Thu, Fri, Sat, Sun
11 Feb 08–17 Feb 08 10:30am–5pm Mon–Sun
18 Feb 08–29 Feb 08 10:30am–4:30pm Wed, Thu, Fri, Sat, Sun

Reserve
All year Dawn–dusk Mon–Sun

BACK TO NATURE

The National Trust protects many areas that are official Nature Reserves or National Nature Reserves. These areas need special protection because many of the species and creatures in them are endangered by development and pollution. Visiting our nature reserves can give your family a wonderful insight into how humans and nature need to co-exist. And besides, these beautiful areas are such wonderful places to enjoy at any time of year – take your binoculars, put on your walking shoes or wellies and get back to nature!

As old as the hills (or fens...)

Many nature reserves are the last remnants of lands that have been nearly lost to development and the spread of human habitation. **Ulverscroft**, in Leicestershire, is part of an ancient forest with a beautiful bluebell season. **Wicken Fen** in Cambridgeshire is an ancient area of fenland with wild ponies, rare butterflies and, if you're lucky, a sighting of an otter or two. **Crom Estate** is an area with tranquil islands, woodland and rare pine martens – one of the Trust's most important reserves. There are little pockets of ancient woodland all over, like **Curbridge** in Hampshire, often within the parklands of the many historic houses owned by the Trust. Visiting these magical places reminds us of what we've lost and need to preserve.

Coastal beauty

Murlough National Nature Reserve, near Newcastle, was Ireland's first national nature reserve, and offers some lovely boarded walkways to the dunes. **Orford Ness** in Suffolk is a National Nature Reserve on the wild and remote extremity of eastern England. This fascinating saltmarsh area also has an interesting military history to explore, having once been an important radar site.

At **Blakeney Point** in Norfolk, you can enjoy an undeveloped coastal area that's noted for its colonies of breeding terns and migrant birds. You can also get a close-up look at seals, both common and grey. **Studland Beach & Nature Reserve** in Dorset is noted for its sandy beaches, but you may also sight seabirds diving into the waves, deer in the dunes and even lizards and snakes. You can take a peek at rare birds from the bird hides at **Little Sea** or learn more from the visitor centre. Quite a few nature reserves have bird hides, like those at **Malham Tarn Estate** in North Yorkshire.

If sea birds, including puffins, take your fancy, you can get close to them at **Farne Islands** in Northumberland and enjoy a bracing boat trip there and back. But wear a hat – our terns are not fussy about who they poo on!

Nearer than you think

Not all nature reserves are in areas of wild or remote countryside – far from it. Many are an oasis of unspoilt natural habitat near to cities and other urban places. **Leigh Woods** near Bristol is a National Nature Reserve that has access for buggies and wheelchairs, and **Hatfield**

Forest is a rare surviving example of a medieval hunting forest in Essex, not that far from London.

And some nature reserves are small, but no less exciting or important. How about **Boarstall Duck Decoy** in Buckinghamshire, a rare survival of a 17th-century decoy beside a lake (complete with trained dog to get the ducks!).

Rare treasures

Today there are only around 160,000 red squirrels in Britain – not that many in the grand scheme of things. The National Trust has four sites that are a haven for these busy little bushy-tailed creatures – **Brownsea Island** in Dorset, **Formby** in Merseyside, **Wallington** in Northumberland and the **Isle of Wight.** Look out for our guided walks and special events when we celebrate 'Red Squirrel Week' each year in September.

While squirrels are cute little animals, the special natural places that the Trust cares for are home to so many other interesting little bugs and birds – from ant-lions to natterjack toads. And the plants and flowers you'll find range from miniature orchids to imposing skunk cabbage. Come outside and enjoy our special places.

Many of our nature reserves and other wildlife areas have Visitor Centres where you can find out much more about what you're seeing (and hearing) in nature. Look us up on our website at **www.nationaltrust.org.uk** to find out what natural wonders are near to you.

Wimpole Home Farm

Park Farm

Wimpole Hall, Arrington,
Royston, Cambridgeshire,
SG8 0BW. 01223 206000

OPENING TIMES
3 Mar–11 Mar 11am–4pm Sat,
Sun
17 Mar–18 Jul 10:30am–5pm
Mon, Tue, Wed, Sat, Sun
21 Jul–30 Aug 10:30am–5pm
Mon, Tue, Wed, Thu, Sat, Sun
1 Sep–31 Oct 10:30am–5pm
Mon, Tue, Wed, Sat, Sun
3 Nov–23 Dec 11am–4pm Sat,
Sun
29 Dec–2 Jan 08 11am–4pm
Mon, Tue, Wed, Sat, Sun
5 Jan 08–24 Feb 08
11am–4pm Sat, Sun

Notes
Under 3s free

Lots to see at this charming farm built by Sir John Soane in 1794 for the 3rd Earl of Hardwicke, who was potty about animals and agriculture. Wimpole is a working farm that's home to all types of rare breeds, which you can look at, touch and even feed. Nearby Wimpole Hall is also worth a visit, with a huge park to explore.

Come in number five!

If you come to Wimpole in April you'll see new-born lambs, and might even see one being born. Once the lambs are born, we give them trendy ear tags (they don't mind them!) and mum and her lambs all have the same number sprayed on their sides, so we know who belongs to who.

What to see

- Different breeds of sheep with strange names like Logthan, Soays, Portland's and Manx.
- Cows, pigs, goats, rabbits, chickens... a farm full of four-legged friends (and two-legged ones with beaks).
- Thatched buildings and a Victorian Dairy.

What to do

- Go on a wagon ride between Home Farm and Wimpole Hall, pulled by our lovely big shire horses – they're such gentle giants.
- Feed the goats or other animals – but don't bring food, buy special food from the shop (better for their tums).
- Cuddle a bunny in the corner for younger children with smaller animals, rabbits and guinea pigs.

Special events

Wimpole Home Farm has many events, like lambing weekends, children's days and Meet Father Christmas. You can even have your birthday party here – just don't share your cake with the chickens! Visit our website or give us a call.

By the way...

- Pushchairs and back-carriers welcome, and there is a children's play area.
- Book one of our 3 wheelchairs and bear in mind that there are some gravel areas.

Woolsthorpe Manor

Historic house Garden Farm Discovery centre

23 Newton Way,
Woolsthorpe-by-Colsterworth,
nr Grantham,
Lincolnshire, NG33 5NR
01476 860338

OPENING TIMES

House/grounds
17 Mar–25 Mar 1pm–5pm Sat,
Sun
28 Mar–30 Sep 1pm–5pm
Wed, Thu, Fri, Sat, Sun
6 Oct–28 Oct 1pm–5pm Sat,
Sun

The birthplace and family home of Sir Isaac Newton, the chap who discovered gravity when an apple fell on his head in this very garden. The apple tree's no more, though one of its descendants lives on. It's amazing to think that Newton had some of his most important and famous ideas in this modest little house.

Irritating Isaac

Newton may have been a clever-clogs but he was also known to be a bit cross and cantankerous. He was prone to disagree with royal astronomers, and had an argument with famous mathematician Leibniz that lasted over 15 years. Well, nobody said a genius has to be nice.

What to see

- A big display telling the story of the discovery of gravity. That's heavy!
- An edition of Newton's famous work Principia, first published in 1687. That's quite heavy too.
- All kinds of Newtonian gadgets in the shop.

What to do

- Wander around the orchards and paddocks.
- Visit the farm buildings with rare breed Lincoln Longwool sheep.
- Dip into the Science Discovery Centre, with a chance to look through telescopes, play with pendulums and more.

Special events

We have an apple day (well, we would...) and have had family learning days that take you back to the 17th century. Get in touch to see what's coming up.

By the way...

- There's a family guide and quiz/trail for you to have a go at. And pick up a leaflet to do a village walk.
- Baby-changing facilities, but bear in mind the café is small and has a limited selection (it's only open at weekends, too).
- You can book a wheelchair, though there are stairs to the upper floors.

Attingham Park

Historic house Park Farm

An elegant 18th-century mansion with a grand façade and swanky Regency interiors – originally the home of the 1st Lord Berwick. See how the other half lived as you admire the silver, furniture and paintings here. The park is also pretty grand, with nice river walks, a play area – and there's also Home Farm, on the edge of the estate.

Bigging it up...
There were lots of tricks to make the house seem bigger! The drive is winding, and goes by especially positioned trees, so that the grounds seem larger. The Main Drawing Room has mirrors at either end, to make the room go on forever. And there are false doors to give the illusion of extra rooms.

What to see
- The Boudoir Room – for the ladies to retreat to. Round and with 5 doors (2 fakes!), it is decorated with romantic cupids.
- The Picture Gallery by John Nash. Look at the picture of Queen Charlotte, whose face ages as you walk past it from left to right.
- The Octagon Room – once Lord Berwick's private 'quiet room'.

What to do
- Imagine being a servant who had to answer when one of the bells in the Bell Room went off – there was one for every room in the house!
- Hunt out the biggest salmon ever caught in Britain in the Tenant's Parlour.
- Dress up, learn to lay a fire or play games of the times in the Family Activity Room.

Special events
Food fayres, deer park rides and carriage parades are just some of our recent events, as well as special activities during holiday times. Get in touch!

By the way...
- There's a children's play area, baby-changing and feeding facilities and you can borrow a child sling. Children's menu in the tea-room.
- Visit the Environmental discovery room in the park to find out about the deer and birds.
- Ask for the alternative entrance if you have mobility problems, and we have wheelchairs available. A handling collection is available, and there are things to touch in the house.

Shrewsbury,
Shropshire, SY4 4TP
01743 708162

OPENING TIMES

House
3 Mar–25 Mar 1pm–5pm Sat, Sun
26 Mar–30 Oct 1pm–5pm Mon, Tue, Fri, Sat, Sun

Deer park
1 Mar–30 Oct 10am–5pm Mon–Sun
2 Nov–29 Feb 08 10am–5pm Mon, Tue, Fri, Sat, Sun

Shop/tea-room
3 Mar–25 Mar 11:30am (10:30 tea-room) –5pm Sat, Sun
26 Mar–30 Oct 11:30am (10:30 tea-room)–5pm Mon, Tue, Fri, Sat, Sun
3 Nov–29 Feb 08 11:30am–4pm Sat, Sun

The Carriage House Kiosk
26 Mar–30 Oct 10:30am–5pm Wed, Thu, Sat, Sun

87

Baddesley Clinton

Historic house Garden Park Lake

Rising Lane, Baddesley
Clinton Village,
Knowle, Solihull, Warwickshire,
B93 0DQ
01564 783294

OPENING TIMES

House
28 Feb–29 Apr 1:30pm–5pm
Wed, Thu, Fri, Sat, Sun
2 May–30 Sep 1:30pm–5:30pm
Wed, Thu, Fri, Sat, Sun
3 Oct–4 Nov 1:30pm–5pm
Wed, Thu, Fri, Sat, Sun

Grounds/shop/restaurant
28 Feb–29 Apr 12–5pm Wed,
Thu, Fri, Sat, Sun
2 May–30 Sep 12–5:30pm
Wed, Thu, Fri, Sat, Sun
3 Oct–4 Nov 12–5pm Wed,
Thu, Fri, Sat, Sun
7 Nov–16 Dec 12–4pm Wed,
Thu, Fri, Sat, Sun

In Elizabethan times this house was riddled with secret hidey-holes to conceal the hounded Catholic Ferrers family and their friends. See if you can spot them, then stretch your legs on the many walks and trails in the grounds.

Not the most pleasant paddle

When Protestant Elizabeth I was on the throne, the house became a refuge for Catholic priests on the run. In 1591 a priest's hole in the drains saved nine Catholic priests, who stood knee-deep in water while the Queen's soldiers searched the house.

What to see

- The Ferrers family coat of arms in the 16th-century stained glass.
- Look carefully by the library fireplace to find a bloodstain from a murder that took place in 1483. Listen carefully too, for ghostly whispering!
- A 16th-century garderobe or loo, that hides the entrance to one of the secret hiding places.

What to do

- Find another priest's hole — ask a steward to help you find it!
- Have a look at the moat — but watch out, don't fall in!
- Listen out for the chiming turret clock, and cosy up to our log fire in March and October.

Special events
Typical events are Bug Hunts, Easter egg trails and other family
activities – get in touch!

By the way...
- The public bridleway is also a cycle path.
- We can loan you a baby or infant sling, and we have changing
  facilities, level entrance and 4 wheelchairs available. Some stairs.

Berrington Hall

Historic house Garden

nr Leominster,
Herefordshire, HR6 0DW
01568 615721

OPENING TIMES
House
3 Mar–18 Mar 1pm–5pm Sat,
Sun
19 Mar–4 Nov 1pm–5pm Mon,
Tue, Wed, Sat, Sun

Garden/shop/tea-room
3 Mar–18 Mar 11am–5pm Sat,
Sun
29 Mar–4 Nov 11am–5pm
Mon, Tue, Wed, Sat, Sun

Park walk
16 Jun–4 Nov 11am–5pm Sat,
Sun
1 Dec–16 Dec 12–4:30pm
Mon, Tue, Wed, Sat, Sun

Wander around inside this elegant late 18th-century house designed by Henry Holland, with its nursery, Victorian laundry and Georgian dairy. Or stroll in the equally attractive gardens designed by 'Capability' Brown, with sweeping views to the Brecon Beacons.

Dressing up
Flip through this book to the page on Snowshill Manor, and you'll realise why Charles Wade didn't have room for his costume collection there. A lot of it is housed here instead, and some is always on display.

What to see
- Two commodes in the very elegant white and gold drawing room (not very private!).
- Dolls and dolls' houses and a lovely rocking chair in the Victorian nursery.

What to do
- Visit the children's play area or try out the children's quiz.
- Hands-on activities arranged most weekends during the season.

Special events
Family activity days, annual Plant Fair, Second World War weekend & Apple Weekend. Get in touch for details of special activities during holidays.

By the way...
- There's a lovely living willow tunnel in the children's play area.
- Baby-changing facilities, and baby slings for loan.
- We have wheelchairs, but should warn you that there are many steps to enter the house.

Brockhampton Estate

Historic house Garden Park Countryside Farm

This fairytale medieval moated manor house has a lovely crooked gatehouse and ruined Norman chapel and is set in extensive areas of woods and traditionally farmed land. We're sure there are some tree sprites in the garden – there are certainly some fun wooden sculptures on the woodland walks.

That's a Great Hall
Inside the house you can see an immense Great Hall, open up to the rafters – and they're made from wood from the estate. Many of those ancient oaks and beeches are still standing.

What to see
- Harold the Shire – a full-size replica shire horse made from a windblown oak.
- In the house, spot a carved wooden lion, and leather fire buckets from the 19th century.
- Sculptures showing scenes from working life in the past.

What to do
- Follow the Nursery Rhyme trail or visit the wildflower meadow.
- Take one of the waymarked walks – Ash, Holly, Beech or Oak. Dogs can come too, under strict control.
- Buy local crafts and produce from The Granary at Lower Brockhampton.

By the way...
- Wonderful place for picnics.
- Farm tours and guided walks by arrangement.
- Pushchairs admitted. Fairly accessible, but parkland can be uneven and muddy so watch out.

Greenfields, Bringsty,
nr Bromyard,
Worcestershire WR6 5TB.
01885 482077

Central

OPENING TIMES
Estate
All year daylight Mon–Sun

House
3 Mar–1 Apr 12pm–4pm Sat, Sun
4 Apr–30 Sep 12pm–5pm Wed, Thu, Fri, Sat, Sun
3 Oct–28 Oct 12pm–4pm Wed, Thu, Fri, Sat, Sun

Tea-room
As house Wed, Thu, Fri, Sat, Sun except
1 Jul–29 Feb 08 12pm–5pm Mon–Sun
1 Dec–31 Dec 12pm–4pm Sat, Sun

Calke Abbey

Historic house Garden Park Farm Nature reserve

Ticknall, Derby,
Derbyshire, DE73 1LE
01332 863822

OPENING TIMES

House
17 Mar–28 Oct 12:30–5pm
Mon, Tue, Wed, Sat, Sun

Garden
17 Mar–28 Oct 11am–5pm
Mon, Tue, Wed, Sat, Sun
5 Jul–7 Sep 11am–5pm
Mon–Sun

Restaurant/shop
17 Mar–28 Oct 10:30am–5pm
Mon, Tue, Wed, Sat, Sun
5 Jul–7 Sep 10:30am–5pm
Mon–Sun
3 Nov–25 Nov 11am–4pm Sat,
Sun
26 Nov–19 Dec 11am–4pm
Mon, Tue, Wed, Sat, Sun
5 Jan 08–29 Feb 08
11am–5pm Sat, Sun

Calke was built in 1701–4 and isn't really an Abbey; for years it was home to the eccentric Harpur Crewe family, who never threw much away. It hasn't changed much since the l880s, and gives an amazing glimpse of 19th-century life. It's also a magical and especially child-friendly place, with some special trails

invisible servants
The owners were a funny lot – they didn't want to see their servants so they built secret corridors and tunnels for them to use. If a servant bumped into a member of the family, they had to turn their face to the wall and pretend to be invisible!

What to see
- Some rather weird collections – cannonballs, shells and stones, and even an alligator skull.
- An aviary with pheasants in it.
- A stunning Chinese silk bed.

What to do
- See how many people you can fit into the hollow tree in the grounds.
- Find the secret walled garden behind a shrubby area.
- Romp around in the grounds – there's a guide to the park.

Special events
Easter Egg hunts, Apple Day, Pumpkin Party and Father Christmas. There's always something special happening at Calke; to find out more please call us.

By the way...

- Calke is very popular, so it can take a while to get in on bank holidays.
- There are wheelchairs available. Quite a lot to see on the ground floor, stairs to the other floors.
- Ask the room steward to show you what items can be touched, or get a list from the entrance hall.
- There's no shaded parking, so think before bringing the dog.

Charlecote Park

Historic house Garden Park Farm

Warwick,
Warwickshire CV35 9ER
07788 658495

OPENING TIMES

House
3 Mar–28 Oct 12–5pm Mon,
Tue, Fri, Sat, Sun
3 Nov–23 Dec 12–4pm Sat,
Sun

Gardens
3 Mar–28 Oct 10:30am–6pm
Mon, Tue, Fri, Sat, Sun
3 Nov–23 Dec 11am–4pm
Sat, Sun

Shop
3 Mar–28 Oct
10:30am–5:30pm Mon, Tue,
Fri, Sat, Sun
3 Nov–23 Dec 11am–4pm
Sat, Sun

Restaurant
3 Mar–28 Oct 10:30am–5pm
Mon, Tue, Fri, Sat, Sun
3 Nov–23 Dec 11am–4pm
Sat, Sun

Park
3 Mar–29 Feb 08 Mon, Tue,
Fri, Sat, Sun

Notes
Croquet set available £3.50
per hour (deposit required)

A grand Tudor house with a landscaped deer park and a formal garden by the River Avon. It's been in the Lucy family for at least 700 years. The imposing Elizabethan gatehouse made from pink brick provides a warm welcome and the rest of the house was largely restored in the 19th century and is in 'Elizabethan Revival' style, complete with ornate ceilings and vaulting.

Deer me
A certain William Shakespeare was allegedly caught poaching in the deer park. Perhaps his plays weren't doing so well at the time. Another famous visitor – this time invited – was Queen Elizabeth I, who stayed at Charlecote for two nights in 1572.

What to see
- A fascinating collection of carriages and other vehicles.
- Look out for the Lucy family's symbol – a fish – it's all around the house.
- Elizabethan stained glass windows in the Great Hall, and a famous table covered with marbles and semi-precious stones.

What to do
- Visit the Victorian kitchen and scullery, the laundry room and the brew-house – kitted out with original equipment like washtubs and vats.
- Spot herds of red and fallow deer roaming capably in 'Capability' Brown's parkland.
- Or explore the children's maze in the play area, with carved wooden deer.

Special events
We cater well for families, and have had bat walks, kite festivals, spinning and weaving demos as well as storytelling and spooky Halloween activities. Get in touch!

By the way...
- There's a ramped entrance, and the ground floor is accessible. We've wheelchairs you can borrow.
- Baby-changing facilities, and carriers for loan, and a children's menu in the restaurant.

Clumber Park

Garden Park Countryside

Clamber around Clumber and you'll find 1540 hectares (3800 acres) of woods, open heath and rolling farmland. In the middle is a superb serpentine lake. Formerly home to the Duke of Newcastle, the house was demolished in 1938 but there is still a chapel and a fascinating walled kitchen garden with some spectacular glass houses.

How many dukes does it take to change a lightbulb?
Can't help you there, but we do know that the district is called 'The Dukeries' because it once had five ducal residences: the Dukes of Newcastle, Kingston, Portland, Norfolk and Leeds. Clumber was the estate of the Dukes of Newcastle for nearly 300 years.

What to see
- The longest greenhouse owned by the NT – that's 137 metres (450 feet) long.
- The longest avenue of lime trees in Europe – that's 3 kilometres (2 miles).
- Clumber Chapel, made as a mini Gothic cathedral – that's small.

What to do
- Whether it be cycling, orienteering or a gentle walk through the park with your dog, Clumber offers it all.
- Those less active can picnic, shop, find out more about Clumber's wildlife in the Conservation Centre where you can stick your hands in the feeling box or simply enjoy the views over refreshments in our catering facilities.

Special events
Organised throughout the year, please contact the Estate Office.

By the way...
- Wheelchairs and PMVs are available. Adapted cycles, tandems and trikes can be hired. There is a ramped entrance to the chapel and the garden.

The Estate Office, Clumber Park, Worksop, Nottinghamshire, S80 3AZ
01909 476592

OPENING TIMES

Park
All year Daylight Mon–Sun

Kitchen garden
31 Mar–30 Sep 10am–6pm Sat, Sun
2 Apr–28 Sep 10am–5pm Mon, Tue, Wed, Thu, Fri

Shop/restaurant/plant sales
31 Mar–30 Sep 10am–6pm Sat, Sun
2 Apr–28 Sep 10am–5pm Mon, Tue, Wed, Thu, Fri
1 Oct–29 Feb 08 10am–4pm Mon–Sun

Notes
Vehicle entry charge: £4.50 per vehicle. Coaches, cyclists and pedestrians free. **Walled Kitchen Garden**: £2, child free. Orienteering by arrangement (orienteering packs £1.95). Horse riding by permit only, £7.50 day permit or £60 annual season ticket. Coarse fishing: 16 June to 14 March, 7am–dusk; £4.50 day ticket or £55 annual season ticket (concessions £2.50/£35)

Central

Croome Park

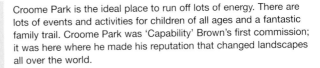
Garden Park Countryside

Croome D'Abitot,
Worcestershire
01905 371006

OPENING TIMES
2 Mar–29 Apr 10am–5:30pm
Wed, Thu, Fri, Sat, Sun
30 Apr–2 Sep 10am–5:30pm
Mon–Sun
5 Sep–28 Oct 10am–5:30pm
Wed, Thu, Fri, Sat, Sun
1 Nov–31 Dec 10am–4pm Sat,
Sun

Croome Park is the ideal place to run off lots of energy. There are lots of events and activities for children of all ages and a fantastic family trail. Croome Park was 'Capability' Brown's first commission; it was here where he made his reputation that changed landscapes all over the world.

For kids of all ages

In and around the parkland there are many things to see and do. The story of 'Capability' Brown and how he created the park is all brought to life through a wide range of family trails and events. You can also see the role that Croome Park played in the Second World War – our new visitor facilities are in buildings left over from when the estate was part of RAF Defford (opening late spring 07). The buildings are the last remaining set of complete Second World War sick quarters in the UK.

What to see

- The parkland that 'Capability' Brown created has some fantastic features; including a grotto, Temple Greenhouse, Island temple, and eye-catcher follies which are all linked by paths.
- Over the years, lots of wildlife have also made Croome Park their home and through activities, walks and trails this is all brought to life.

What to do

- The family trail is superb fun. Kids are sent on a mission to spy on Lord and Lady Coventry to see how their park was created. The trail takes in the wider parkland, the miles of culverts that feed into the lake and river, the stories of the plant collectors and visitors who used the Pleasure Grounds in Georgian times (we've also included a leaflet for adults to use – just in case you get a little stuck!).
- There is also a walks leaflet which takes in different parts of the park and surrounding areas. Rather than just spot the outer eye-catchers from the park, you can go and visit them instead.

Special events

There's something going on during most weekends. There are lots of
great guided walks – looking at different parts of the park – its wildlife,
trees, nuts and berries. There's hands-on activity events, kite flying, the
annual dog show (Pooches n' Croome) and Trusty the Hedgehog is a
regular visitor. During the summer school holidays we're open every
day – so come along and run around!

By the way...

- We recommend that you wear sturdy shoes.
- The park is very accessible with paths all the way through the
  Pleasure Ground and mown paths through the meadows. You're
  more than welcome to bring a picnic and lay out your rug wherever
  your like – enjoy lunch by the lake or tea by the temple!

Hardwick Hall

Historic house Garden Park Countryside Farm

Doe Lea, Chesterfield,
Derbyshire S44 5QJ
01246 850430

OPENING TIMES

Hall
17 Mar–28 Oct 12–4:30pm
Wed, Thu, Sat, Sun

Garden
17 Mar–28 Oct 11am–5:30pm
Wed, Thu, Fri, Sat, Sun

Parkland gates
All year 8am–6pm Mon–Sun

Old Hall (EH)
17 Mar–28 Oct 10am–6pm
Wed, Thu, Sat, Sun

Shop/restaurant
17 Mar–28 Oct 11am–5pm
Wed, Thu, Sat, Sun

Stone Centre
17 Mar–28 Oct 11am–1pm;
2–4pm Wed, Thu, Sat, Sun

Hardwick Hall is a truly spectacular Tudor house, one of the most complete in Britain. It presides over the Derbyshire countryside with the same grandeur that its builder, Bess of Hardwick, did.

The Queen's rival

Elizabeth Hardwick, known as Bess of Hardwick, was the second most powerful and wealthy woman in Tudor England – she rivalled Queen Elizabeth I. Ambitious in her choice of husbands, she even married off one of her daughters to Charles Stuart, brother of the late husband of Mary Queen of Scots, who had both Royal Tudor and Stuart blood in his veins. Their daughter, Arbelle Stuart, was in direct line for the throne of England.

What to see

- See how this powerful Tudor aristocrat would have lived – Hardwick remains virtually unchanged since Bess lived here
- Learn about the rare breeds of sheep and cattle.
- Visit the 'Threads of Time' exhibition.
- Outstanding 16th- and 17th-century tapestries and embroideries.

What to do

- Have a picnic in the stunning parkland.
- Take a walk around the Elizabethan walled courtyards, visit the orchard and spot different apple varieties.
- Take a tour of the stonemason's yard.
- There are lots of events held every year, so phone up and ask: search through the undergrowth on a Fungi Foray, dress up as a witch for Halloween and take part in the Bat Hunt or Pumpkin competition or go on a haunted tour of the house.

Special events
Easter Egg trails, Family Fun days, Elizabethan weekend, Costume Days, Halloween activities.

Kedleston Hall

Historic house Garden Park Lake

A really sumptuous Palladian mansion, built between 1759 and 1765 for the Curzon family. Magnificent state rooms designed by Robert Adams, loads of paintings, a museum with weird objects from Lord Curzon's Indian travels, and walks in the restored 18th-century 'pleasure grounds' – complete with a lake and cascades. A very grand day out with lots to enjoy.

Out of my way!
Sir Nathaniel Curzon, who inherited Kedleston in 1758, thought the village spoilt the view from where he wanted his new house to go. So he had the village moved, stone by stone. What a nerve!

What to see
- Curious trompe l'oeil paintings that can fool you into thinking they're 3-D.
- A summer house and numerous sculptures hiding in the grounds,
- A model of the Taj Mahal in the Eastern Museum.

What to do
- Count the amazing alabaster columns in the Marble Hall as you go inside the house. Then look up at that ceiling – wow!
- Look out for the grand bed decorated with ostrich feathers.
- Have a go at the children's quiz.

Special events
Contact us for details. In the past we've had children's theatre shows, spinning demonstrations and craft workshops.

By the way...
- The parkland is a great place to romp, and dogs on leads are welcome.
- There's an alternative entrance avoiding the steps, and we have wheelchairs available. The upper floor has a flight of 22 steps.
- We can loan you a hip-carrying infant seat, and there are baby-changing facilities and a children's menu in the restaurant.

Derby,
Derbyshire, DE22 5JH
01332 842191

OPENING TIMES

House
10 Mar–31 Oct 12am–4:30pm
Mon, Tue, Wed, Sat, Sun

Garden
10 Mar–31 Oct 10am–6pm
Mon–Sun

Park
10 Mar–31 Oct 10am–6pm
Mon–Sun
1 Nov–29 Feb 08 10am–4pm
Mon–Sun

Shop
10 Mar–31 Oct 11am–5pm
Mon, Tue, Wed, Sat, Sun
21 Jul–24 Aug 12–4pm Thu, Fri
3 Nov–29 Feb 08 12–4pm Sat, Sun

Restaurant
10 Mar–31 Oct 11am–5pm
Mon, Tue, Wed, Sat, Sun
21 Jul–24 Aug 12–4pm Thu, Fri
3 Nov–29 Feb 08 12–4pm Sat, Sun

Church
10 Mar–31 Oct 11am–5pm
Mon, Tue, Wed, Sat, Sun

Notes
(Park & garden ticket refundable against tickets for house)

Central

Shugborough Estate

Historic house Mill Garden Park Countryside Farm

Central

Milford, nr Stafford,
Staffordshire, ST17 0XB
01889 881388

OPENING TIMES
**House/farm/servants'
quarters/grounds/tea-room**
16 Mar–27 Oct 11am–5pm
Mon–Sun

Shop
16 Mar–27 Oct 11am–5pm
Mon–Sun
28 Oct–23 Dec 11am–4pm
Mon–Sun

The complete working historic estate of Shugborough where you can get stuck in... cheese-making, dolly-pegging, baking, milling, mangling, growing, tasting, exploring. Shugborough, set in 900 acres of great, open grassy spaces and gardens is the perfect place to let the whole family loose to enjoy a fun day out packed with living history.

Ahhhh!
The farm at Shugborough has been going since 1805 and is home to some rare breed farm animals, like Snowdrop the miniature Dexter cow. Her baby calf was only 30 centimetres (12 inches) tall when he was born! Meet Mrs Wheelock at the farm who always needs a hand baking for the hungry estate workers. Roll up your sleeves and help out in the dairy before meeting the miller, William Bailey, who will be happy to show off his working water mill. No visit to the farm would be complete without meeting the animals and there's Pudding the donkey, Iris the cow, Patch and Bluey the rabbits to name but a few.

What to see
- A fun ride on Lucy the train will take you to the Servants' Quarters. There, head cook Mrs Stearn is waiting in the gigantic old kitchen making sure visitors' nails are clean and hair tidy before they are set to work. Remember to ask her what she uses for a fridge!
- In the laundry there's loads going on as the maids are hard at work on wash day, mangling, scrubbing and dolly-pegging.

What to do
- Have a go on the children's adventure playground, and climb aboard Lucy the train for a free ride from the ticket office to the farm.
- Try and crack the code under the 'Shepherds' monument in the grounds. Nobody has yet!
- Watch the working historic watermill in action.
- The fine Mansion House is massive with loads of rooms filled with treasure. Costumed characters Lord and Lady Anson are probably in residence so be on your best behaviour!
- Have lunch in our tea-rooms and try the weird-sounding courgette and chocolate cake. It's delicious and a favourite with kids.
- Meet the gardeners in the Walled Garden, they will be chatting to visitors and might ask you to help out digging and planting the beds using old tools.

Special events

There is a range of events throughout the year from our Easter Eggstravaganza to Family Fun Bank Holidays in May, Historic Food Fayres and spectacular Christmas Evenings – when it always snows!

By the way...

- Baby changing and feeding facilities. Hip-carrying infant seats for loan.
- Children's play area.
- Farm gives children a chance to see domestic and rare breeds of animal and poultry.
- Games gallery in corn mill plus children's guide and quiz. The 'first person' guides and experiences are unique and the children love it.
- Pushchairs admitted to farm.

Snowshill Manor

House   Garden   Collections

Snowshill, nr Broadway,
Worcestershire, WR12 7JU
01386 852410

OPENING TIMES
House
24 Mar–28 Oct 12–5pm Wed,
Thu, Fri, Sat, Sun

Garden
24 Mar–28 Oct 11am–5:30pm
Wed, Thu, Fri, Sat, Sun

Shop/restaurant
24 Mar–28 Oct 11am–5:30pm
Wed, Thu, Fri, Sat, Sun
4 Nov–9 Dec 12–4pm Sat, Sun

Notes
Visitors arriving by bicycle or on
foot offered a voucher
redeemable at Snowshill NT
shop or tea-room

This is the house of architect and craftsman Charles Paget Wade, who was a passionate collector. There are over 5000 objects to peruse, from Samurai warriors to spinners' tools. The organic garden is just as eccentric, with a magical combination of terraces and ponds forming little outdoor rooms.

Crowded house
Charles just didn't know when to stop – he started collecting at age 7, and by 1919 he had so much stuff in this house that he had to move next door. Have you ever wished you could do that?

What to see
- Musical instruments, clocks, toys, masks.
- Samurai armour, Wade's great-great-grandmother's barrel organ.
- Bicycles in the room of One Hundred Wheels.
- Model ships in every spare space. And that's just for starters…

What to do
- Explore the rooms each named by Wade to reflect what is in them – our favourite: Seventh Heaven and Dragon.
- Pick up a children's discovery sheet and explore the garden, or a quiz sheet in the house.

Special events

Check with us – we've had a Neptune treasure hunt, an Easter bunny trail, Ugly Bug Ball, plus Samurai martial arts groups fighting on the lawn. Who knows what might be on the cards?

By the way...

- Baby-changing facilities. We can loan a baby sling or carrier.
- Please don't take photos without written agreement – ask us first.
- It's a 10-minute walk to the house along a bumpy path. Once inside, we have 2 wheelchairs. Touchable objects and interesting sounds – ask about our handling collection.

Sudbury Hall

Historic house Garden Museum

Sudbury Hall, Ashbourne,
Derbyshire, DE6 5HT
Museum 01283 585337

OPENING TIMES

Hall
10 Mar–28 Oct 1pm–5pm Wed,
Thu, Fri, Sat, Sun

Grounds
10 Mar–28 Oct 10am–6pm
Wed, Thu, Fri, Sat, Sun

Tea-room
10 Mar–28 Oct 11am–5pm
Wed, Thu, Fri, Sat, Sun

Shop
10 Mar–28 Oct 12:30pm–5pm
Wed, Thu, Fri, Sat, Sun

Sudbury Hall will be open as usual and will be enhanced for 2007 with a mini Museum of Childhood created in the basement area (the main Museum is due to re-open in 2008 after extensive refurbishment). The Hall dates back to the late 17th century, and the interiors are exquisite, with fine decorative plasterwork, wood carvings and painted murals.

Recognise anything?
The BBC used some rooms in the Hall to film *Pride and Prejudice* – can you tell which scenes were filmed where? Visitors can also explore the Willow Walk and make their way to the Discovery Centre at the Boat House, picnic on the meadow and watch the swans swim by.

What to see
- Explore the Hall with our new Children's Activity Sheets and Treasure Chests, and pick up a self-guided Garden Trail.

What to do
- Explore our Costume Trail in the Hall from March to the close of August, when you can experience costumes, stitchery and embroidery from various Jane Austen productions. In the Hall, uncover life 'below stairs' with our Meet the Butler tours. Or encounter smells (and feels) of the past in special treasure chests. Explore the mini Museum of Childhood and see our exhibition about the 'new' Museum.

Special events
Join us for family activities and fun in the school holidays and
weekends, Wednesdays to Sundays from 1 to 4pm.

By the way...
- Avoid a dull day if you want to see the paintings clearly as we don't
  have very bright lighting, as we wish people to enjoy the paintings
  and furnishings for a few more hundred years, and light can cause a
  lot of damage.
- Children have to be accompanied by grown-ups... get them to
  explore with you, they will love it, too.

The Workhouse, Southwell

Historic building   Gardens

Upton Road, Southwell,
Nottinghamshire, NG25 0PT
01636 817250

OPENING TIMES
17 Mar–8 Apr 12–5pm Sat, Sun
9 Apr–22 Apr 12–5pm Mon,
Wed, Thu, Fri, Sat, Sun
26 Apr–29 Jul 12–5pm Thu, Fri,
Sat, Sun
30 Jul–31 Aug 12–5pm Mon,
Wed, Thu, Fri, Sat, Sun
1 Sep–28 Sep 12–5pm Thu,
Fri, Sat, Sun
29 Sep–28 Oct 12–5pm Sat,
Sun

Tours
30 Jul–31 Aug 11am–12am
Mon, Wed, Thu, Fri, Sat, Sun

Notes
Introductory video, displays and
audio guide included. **Guided
tours:** £4.50 for NT members,
£5.50 for non-members

The Workhouse is the least altered example of a kind of 'welfare'
brought about by the New Poor Law of 1834. Paupers – poor people
who had no work, or had fallen into debt or disgrace – lived in grim
conditions here. It's worth a visit to see just how life has changed.

Or has it?
You can see a fully recreated 19th-century dormitory with replica beds
here. But next door there is also a re-creation of a bedsit, to remind
you that the building's most recent welfare use was as housing for the
temporarily homeless in the 1970s.

What to see
- A film to start with, where the Reverend Becher will introduce the
  Workhouse and bring it to life.
- The old workshops and dormitories.
- Segregated rooms for women and men — and segregated
  stairways too!

What to do
- Follow the excellent audio guide, which is based on archive records
  and brings the building to life.
- Interact with displays that tell you about poverty through the years.
- Play 'The Master's Punishment' game.

Special events
Rag doll making is held every first Sunday of the month and living history with an accompanying children's trail is held on the third Sunday of the month. Various craft and performance workshops are held throughout the year – call property for details.

By the way...
- There's food in the local villages, but no café on site (it's a very authentic Workhouse!) although you can picnic here.
- Baby-changing facilities and pushchairs are fine, though you can borrow a hip-carrying infant seat.
- Get in touch if you would like to use one of our wheelchairs. It's not suitable for motorised wheelchairs.

Beatrix Potter Gallery

Gallery   Walks

Gallery: Main Street, Hawkshead, Cumbria, LA22 0NS
015394 36355

Hill Top: Near Sawrey, Hawkshead, Ambleside, Cumbria, LA22 0LF
015394 36269

OPENING TIMES

Gallery
3 Mar–25 Mar
10:30am–4:30pm Sat, Sun
31 Mar–27 May
10:30am–4:30pm Mon, Tue, Wed, Sat, Sun
28 May–31 Aug
10:30am–4:30pm Mon, Tue, Wed, Thu, Sat, Sun
1 Sep–21 Oct
10:30am–4:30pm Mon, Tue, Wed, Sat, Sun
22 Oct–28 Oct
10:30am–4:30pm Mon–Sun

Shop
1 Mar–25 Mar 10am–4pm Tue, Fri, Sat, Sun
26 Mar–11 Nov 10am–5pm Mon–Sun
14 Nov–23 Dec 10am–4pm Tue, Fri, Sat, Sun

Notes
Discount for Hill Top ticket holders (not applicable to groups)

Here you'll find a fascinating exhibition on the life of children's author Beatrix Potter, including original illustrations for her books. It's housed inside a 17th-century Lakeland town house that was the model for Tabitha Twitchitt's shop and was once the office of Beatrix's husband, William Heelis.

Hill Top House
The house where Beatrix wrote many of her stories, left much as it was when she lived in it. There's something from one of her books in each room — see if you can spot them. Characters in Beatrix Potter's books like Peter Rabbit and Tom Kitten are based on pets she had as a child. Beatrix had quite a lonely childhood, and was taught at home by a governess, but had many animal friends to keep her company.

What to see
- Watercolours and sketches that Beatrix Potter drew to illustrate her books.
- The lovely Lakeland countryside that inspired her.
- The house she lived in.

What to do
- Pick up a leaflet and take a walk around Beatrix Potter country.
- Try the children's activity sheets and get a goodie bag from the gallery.

Special events
At the gallery we have occasional story reading for families, and special exhibitions.

By the way...
- Sorry, no WC at the gallery. But there's one nearby in the main village car park 200 yards away.
- You do need to manage a flight of stairs to get to the exhibition.
- The house can get extremely busy at holiday times, and sometimes you may not be able to get in if we're full.

Dunham Massey

Historic house Mill Garden Park

Altrincham,
Cheshire, WA14 4SJ
0161 941 1025

OPENING TIMES

House
17 Mar–28 Oct 12–5pm Mon,
Tue, Wed, Sat, Sun

Garden
17 Mar–28 Oct 11am–5:30pm
Mon–Sun

Park
24 Mar–28 Oct 9am–7:30pm
Mon – Sun
29 Oct–29 Feb 08 9am–5pm
Mon – Sun

Restaurant/shop
24 Mar–28 Oct 10:30am–5pm
Mon – Sun
29 Oct–29 Feb 08
10:30am–4pm Mon – Sun

Mill
24 Mar–28 Oct 12am–4pm
Mon, Tue, Wed, Sat, Sun

Outside this is an early Georgian house, built around a Tudor core. Inside, it's a wonderful example of sumptuous Edwardian interior décor, with fascinating servants' quarters. The deer park has beautiful avenues and ponds, and a newly restored Tudor mill in working order. The garden is charming and has an orangery to explore.

Motte or not?
There's a flattened mound in the garden which might be the remains of a Norman motte – an extremely old castle. An 18th-century painting of a bird's-eye view of the garden shows it clearly visible – but rather dressed up, with terraces cut into it and a gilded urn on top.

What to see
- A huge collection of Huguenot silver – the finest in Britain.
- A bark-house and a well-house in the garden.
- The mill; originally it ground corn but now it's a sawmill.

What to do
- Spot the tower and the sundial.
- Pick up a children's quiz/trail.
- Eat your sandwiches in our extensive picnic area – but not in the deer park, please!

Special events
We have family tours and activities and special family activities in the holidays. At Christmas and other times you can experience the hustle and bustle of a Victorian kitchen, or meet the butler face to face – so mind your Ps and Qs! Give us a call for more details.

By the way…
- There are many touchable things, and wonderful scents and sounds in the gardens.
- Although there are a lot of stairs, we do have wheelchairs.
- Baby-changing, child-carrier loan and children's menu available.

110

Fell Foot Park

Park Lake Boats

This wonderful park on the shores of Lake Windermere is open all year round. It doesn't cost a penny to visit, and is a great place for a family afternoon out. You can hire rowing boats to splash about in or take a ferry to Lakeside Pier. Or you can sit back with your picnic and enjoy the view of the Lakeland fells. Sounds OK!

Fell (Feel!) like a bit of history?
Fell Foot Park was once the garden of a big house that has now been demolished. The National Trust is gradually restoring the park to how it was in Victorian times.

What to see
- Go on a (pushchair-friendly) walk to identify monkey puzzle and giant redwood trees.
- Pleasure boats going by on Lake Windemere.

What to do
- Hire a rowing boat — and don't drop the oars!
- Spend the whole day here, swimming and picnicking.
- Go mad on the huge adventure playground, with a special bit for children under seven.

Special events
We have a busy summer activities and events programme including children's open air theatre and Shakespeare in the park. Please call for details.

By the way...
- Always supervise kids while swimming and watch out for danger warnings.
- Staff-driven mobility vehicles are available during the season.
- Trusty the Hedgehog lunch boxes in the licensed tea-rooms.

Newby Bridge, Ulverston, Cumbria, LA12 8NN
015395 31273

North West

OPENING TIMES
Park
All year 9am–5pm Mon–Sun

Shop/tea-room
17 Mar–29 Oct 11am–5pm Mon–Sun

Formby

Countryside Coastline Wood Beach

Victoria Road, Freshfield,
Formby,
Liverpool, L37 1LJ
01704 878591

OPENING TIMES
All year dawn–dusk Mon–Sun

The red squirrels are often easy to see and some may come very close to you on the Squirrel Walk. There are wide sandy beaches ideal for beach games and sandcastles. The landscape is beautiful with high sand dunes and pine woodland.

Squirrel these facts away...
Did you know that the red squirrel is native to Britain, but is being forced out of its natural habitat by the strong American grey squirrel? Red squirrels have sharp ears and a very bushy tail, which they use to steer when they're leaping in the air. They squirrel their food away for the winter, and you can see them sniffing the ground to find it again later.

What to see
- Rare red squirrels chasing each other up and down tall pine trees.
- At low tide search for footprints left by prehistoric humans and wild animals in hard baked mud uncovered by erosion on parts of the beach.
- Wading birds on the shore, like oystercatchers and sanderlings.

What to do
- Sit very still and a squirrel may come very close to you (get some squirrel food from the kiosk).
- Take a paddle in the sea and have a picnic in one of the woodland picnic sites. Enjoy an ice cream from the van.
- Head out on wonderful walks along the improved Sefton Coastal Path – many sections suitable for people of all abilities.

Special events
There are many family-friendly events during the year – phone us for details or see the notice-board.

By the way...
- The beach access has steep sand dunes, not good for people with mobility difficulties.
- Baby-changing facilities. Picnic areas – no barbecues, please.
- A good dog-walking place, but please keep the pooch on the lead in the squirrel walks.

Lyme Park

Historic house Garden Park Countryside

Originally a Tudor house, Lyme Park was transformed into a huge Italianate palace in the 18th century, but some of the Elizabethan interiors remain. The garden has many features to explore, including a ravine garden and a conservatory. And the surrounding 570 hectares (1400 acres) of parkland is a medieval deer park.

Mr Darcy's wet shirt
Lyme Park's starring role came as the place where Darcy (played by actor Colin Firth) emerged from the lake in the 1995 BBC TV version of *Pride and Prejudice*. Other members of the family may be more interested in the adventure playground.

What to see
- Deer in the medieval parkland, which also has an 18th-century hunting tower.
- Paintings of the huge Lyme mastiff hunting dogs bred here and given as presents.
- Intricate wood carvings done by Grinling Gibbons (but not of monkeys...).

What to do
- Explore the moorland and woodland in the park. Dogs can come too if kept under control.
- Visit the Cage, a grand former hunting lodge in the park – used for watching the hunt and for banquets.
- Scramble on the adventure playground.

Special events
We're especially good at weekly holiday activities, and have recently had Boredom Busters – crafts and different things to do each week – and Let's Go Fly a Kite, which speaks for itself. Call for info.

By the way...
- There's an alternative entrance to the house, avoiding steps, and we have wheelchairs. There are stairs, though.
- We're very child-friendly. Baby-changing and feeding facilities, bottle-warming, and slings to borrow. There's also a children's menu in the restaurant.

Disley, Stockport, Cheshire, SK12 2NX. 01663 762023

OPENING TIMES

House
23 Mar–30 Oct 1pm–5pm Mon, Tue, Fri, Sat, Sun

Park
1 Apr–14 Oct 8am–8:30pm Mon–Sun
15 Oct–28 Feb 08 8am–6pm Mon–Sun

Garden
4 Mar–24 Mar 12–3pm Sat, Sun
25 Mar–31 Oct 11am–5pm Mon – Sun
4 Nov–16 Dec 12–3pm Sat, Sun

Shop
25 Mar–31 Oct 11am–5pm Mon – Sun
4 Nov–16 Dec 12–4pm Sat, Sun
12 Dec–1 Jan 08 12–4pm Mon, Wed, Thu, Fri, Sat, Sun
6 Jan 08–24 Feb 08 12am–4pm Sat, Sun

Restaurant
25 Mar–30 Oct 11am–5pm Mon, Tue, Fri, Sat, Sun

North West

Quarry Bank Mill and Styal Estate

Mill Countryside Village Living history

Styal, Wilmslow,
Cheshire, SK9 4LA
01625 527468

OPENING TIMES

Mill/shop
19 Mar–1 Oct 11am–5pm Mon
–Sun
2 Oct–28 Feb 08 11am–4pm
Wed, Thu, Fri, Sat, Sun

Apprentice House
19 Mar–1 Oct See below Tue,
Wed, Thu, Fri, Sat, Sun
2 Oct

Estate
All year 7am–6am Mon–Sun

Restaurant
19 Mar–1 Oct 11am–5pm
Mon–Sun
2 Oct–28 Feb 08 11am–4pm
Wed, Thu, Fri, Sat, Sun

Notes
Discounted combined rail, bus
and entry tickets, enquire at
your local station

Where did our great grandparents work? How did they live? Experience something of the noise and hardship in their lives as you trace the story of cotton through the mill. Demonstrators and hands-on exhibits bring the past to life in this unique insight into Britain's industrial heritage.

Home from work
Styal Village was built especially for the people who worked at the mill. The Apprentice House was built as somewhere for the 90 pauper children who worked in the mill to live. No excuse for being late for work...

What to see
- The most powerful working waterwheel in Europe in action – made of iron and huge!
- See demonstrations of spinning and weaving.
- Look.... a long way up the main mill chimney.

What to do
- Go on a tour of the Apprentice House with a costumed guide to learn what conditions were like for children who worked here (limited during term time).
- Watch the two steam engines in the mill that were used from around 1810.
- Pick up a leaflet and take a walk in the woods, or picnic in the Mill meadow.

Special events
Easter egg trails, family activities in the Mill during the school holidays. Telephone for information.

By the way...
- There is a children's play area and baby-changing and feeding facilities. Children's menu during school holidays.
- There are interactive exhibits and opportunities for touching and handling objects.
- Many steps, with handrail, to entrance. A chair lift and wheelchair are available.

Rufford Old Hall

Historic house Garden

The Great Hall looks just like the one on *Scooby Doo* and it's even got the scary suits of armour and lots of weapons. You can take delight at the flowers in the formal garden or let off steam exploring the woods and grounds. You can even watch a narrowboat glide by on the canal and feed the ducks.

Two's company, three's a (ghostly) crowd
Rufford is supposed to be haunted by not one but three ghosts! The 'Grey Lady', a man dressed in Elizabethan clothes, and Queen Elizabeth I — who has been seen pottering about in the dining room, but vanishes if you try to say hello. Well, how rude.

What to see
- The very large Great Hall with an intricate carved screen. Some think Shakespeare acted here.
- Look up to see coats of arms of the powerful local families of the time.
- Wow, those 16th-century suits of armour were small — would they fit Dad?

What to do
- Find the huge fireplace in the Great Hall, where a secret chamber was found—perhaps to hide Catholic priests from sight.
- Enjoy the late-Victorian grounds with topiary and sculpture.
- Have a picnic or enjoy a tasty snack from the Old Kitchen Restaurant.

Special events
In the past we've had magic days, a chance to stroke rescued owls, Tudor games, dancing and more. Get in touch to see what we have planned when you want to visit.

By the way...
- We love kids — baby-changing facilities, slings for loan. A bottle-warming service, and Early Learning toys to play with.
- Allow time; the car park can get very busy.
- Tie Rover up outside the shop; we'll provide fresh water for hot dogs.
- There are wheelchairs, but some steps inside. Everywhere else is pretty accessible with a bit of help from a friend.

200 Liverpool Road,
Rufford, nr Ormskirk,
Lancashire L40 1SG
01704 821254

OPENING TIMES

Garden/shop/restaurant
10 Mar–18 Mar 12–4pm Sat, Sun

House
24 Mar–28 Oct 1pm–5pm Mon, Tue, Wed, Sat, Sun

Garden
24 Mar–28 Oct 11am–5:30pm Mon, Tue, Wed, Sat, Sun

Shop/restaurant
24 Mar–28 Oct 11am–5pm Mon, Tue, Wed, Sat, Sun

Garden/shop/restaurant
28 Oct–16 Dec 12–4pm Wed, Thu, Fri, Sat, Sun

Speke Hall, Gardens & Estate

Historic house Garden Countryside Moat

The Walk,
Liverpool, L24 1XD
0151 427 7231

OPENING TIMES

House
17 Mar–28 Oct 1pm–5:30pm
Wed, Thu, Fri, Sat, Sun
3 Nov–2 Dec 1pm–4:30pm Sat,
Sun

Grounds
17 Mar–28 Oct 11am–5:30pm
Mon–Sun
3 Nov–28 Feb 08 11–dusk
Mon–Sun

Home Farm/restaurant/shop
17 Mar–15 Jul 11am–5pm
Wed, Thu, Fri, Sat, Sun
17 Jul–9 Sep 11am–5pm Tue,
Wed, Thu, Fri, Sat, Sun
12 Sep–28 Oct 11am–5pm
Wed, Thu, Fri, Sat, Sun
3 Nov–2 Dec 11am–4:30pm
Sat, Sun

One of the most famous Tudor manors in Britain, this rambling pile has an atmospheric interior that covers many periods. The oldest parts date from 1530, but there is also a fully equipped Victorian kitchen, not to mention William Morris wallpapers in some rooms.

Only in America
There is a copy of the Hall in California, built in 1912 as a weekend getaway by Percy T. Morgan, and designed to withstand earthquakes. The Tudors would be proud!

What to see
- The 19th-century 'thunderbox' loo. This was supposed to be an improvement on the rather basic Tudor garderobes, but both designs 'deposit' straight into the moat ... hmm.
- Adam and Eve, two majestic Yew trees, which are as old as the house.
- Also a spy-hole in one of the bedrooms.

What to do
- Search for the secret priest's hole. The Norris family, who lived here, were Catholics, at a time when it was against the law.
- Visit the Home Farm visitor centre, with a children's play area and picnic space. It was originally a 'model farm' (a small farm but with real animals).
- Walk through the gardens to the 'Bund', an earth bank, offering views of Liverpool Airport and the Mersey Estuary.

Special events
We have events for all the family including Easter trails, outdoor theatre, Halloween and costumed tours.

By the way...
- Baby-changing facilities. We can loan a baby sling or carrier. Children's menu in Home Farm restaurant.
- Dogs on lead – but in the grounds only, please.
- You can book a wheelchair, and there's a vehicle to take people from Home Farm to the house – they're a short distance apart.

Wordsworth House

Historic house Garden

William Wordsworth's childhood home has much to interest families, with a working Georgian kitchen, items to touch and use, and servants to encounter. This can give insight into children's lives 230 years ago.

Family poetry
William lived here with his three bothers and sister Dorothy for his first eight years. He later referred to this period in his poetry, especially the garden terrace walk which overlooks the River Derwent.

What to see
- Observe the servants' daily routine: the workings of the Georgian kitchen can be explained by the maid-of-all-work while she is cooking; the nursemaid may be making the children's bed or spinning; and the manservant may be setting the dining table.
- Historic varieties of plants in the walled garden, which supplies the house with flowers, fruit, herbs and vegetables.

What to do
- Play with replicas of 1770s toys and try on clothing in the children's bedroom.
- Try writing with a quill pen under supervision of the clerk
- Read some of William's poetry.

Special events
Easter Trail in the garden. Free children's activities in the school holidays eg: poetry competition, making posies or pastry fish, or skittles.

By the way...
- There is a small grassed area for picnics. Refreshments are available from nearby cafés

Main Street, Cockermouth, Cumbria CA13 9RX
01900 824805

North West

OPENING TIMES

House
27 Mar–30 Jun 11am–4:30pm
Tue, Wed, Thu, Fri, Sat
2 Jul–31 Aug 11am–4:30pm
Mon, Tue, Wed, Thu, Fri, Sat
1 Sep–27 Oct 11am–4:30pm
Tue, Wed, Thu, Fri, Sat

Shop
7 Mar–24 Mar 10am–5pm Mon, Tue, Wed, Thu, Fri, Sat
26 Mar–23 Dec 10am–4pm Wed, Thu, Fri, Sat
2 Jan 08–26 Feb 08 Wed, Thu, Fri, Sat

Notes
Additional charges may apply for some living history activities for groups out of hours. Reciprocal ticket available from Wordsworth House allows visitors to enjoy Dove Cottage and Rydal Mount (nr Grasmere, not NT) at reduced rates.

A-MAZING MAZES

Pardon the pun, but some of our mazes are truly a-mazing! If you want a bit of exercise with some puzzling thrown in, then a maze is for you. And we have all kinds at our properties, from easy ground-level decorative mazes to mazes with tall hedges and complicated patterns.

Get me out of here!

Getting in and out of a maze is easier than you think. When you go in, all you have to do in order to get to the middle is to put a hand out to one side (left or right – but stick to whichever you choose!). Keep your hand on the hedge as you walk around. You mustn't lose contact – even if it leads you up a blind alley first. In a real maze, this is guaranteed to get you to the centre. And just do the process in reverse to get out again. Easy!

But remember, if you get stuck – yelling can help too!

What are mazes for?

Mazes are beautiful garden features in themselves, and were an elegant way for people to take exercise. In earlier times, when meeting your beloved in private wasn't that easy – perhaps they were good places to sneak off for a cuddle! But mazes have strong historical and religious roots, too. Some are thought to be ancient symbols, and in the Middle Ages mazes were inlaid on church floors – not very hard to get out of! Some think that people followed them as a kind of worship, by walking or even kneeling as they went round in prayer.

We don't have any like that, but there's a maze made from cobbles at **Peckover House** in Cambridgeshire on the site of the earlier hedge maze. Don't go around on your knees, though! While you're there, why not hire equipment to play croquet on the lawn?

Grassy puzzles

Turf or grass mazes are simply cut into the grass, and may go back to Roman times. They may have just been to entertain people. **East Riddlesden Hall** in Yorkshire has a grass maze that's certainly fun to explore, and another maze without high hedges is the Archbishop's Maze at **Greys Court**, in Oxfordshire – no chance of getting lost, but a great brain-teaser.

Those grand mazes with hedges were all the rage in 16th-century England. National Trust properties with impressive hedge mazes include **Glendurgan Garden** in Cornwall, with a laurel maze 1-metre (3ft 4in) high (as well as the fantastic 'Giant's Stride' maypole) and **Kedleston Hall** in Derbyshire. At Kedleston the maze is planted from beautiful beech hedges – it's still quite young, so you may be able to peek over at the moment!

Animal amazement

Mazes are still used in science: everyone knows the maze that white mice get popped into, to try and find their way to food. We won't make you follow a maze to get to your lunch, but our maze at **Charlecote Park** in Warwickshire has some deer – of the carved wood variety.

And, finally – it's even more a-Maize-ing!

Sorry, we just couldn't help that pun to finish with. But do try out the big maize maze at **Speke Hall**, near Liverpool – it's only there in the summer and is very impressive. Not sure what happens to all the maize afterwards, but perhaps you liked our corn-y jokes about it.

See National Trust web page **www.nationaltrust.org.uk** and other entries in this book for more information on opening times and admission.

Charlecote Park
Warwick, Warwickshire,
CV35 9ER

East Riddlesden Hall
Bradford Road, Keighley,
West Yorkshire, BD20 5EL

Glendurgan Garden
Mawnan Smith, nr Falmouth,
Cornwall, TR11 5JZ

Greys Court
Rotherfield Greys,
Henley-on-Thames,
Oxfordshire, RG9 4PG

Kedleston Hall
Derby, Derbyshire, DE22 5JH

Peckover House & Garden
North Brink, Wisbech,
Cambridgeshire, PE13 1JR

Speke Hall, Garden & Estate
The Walk, Liverpool, L24 1XD

Beningbrough Hall & Gardens

Historic house Garden

Beningbrough, York,
North Yorkshire YO30 1DD.
01904 472027

OPENING TIMES

Grounds/shop/restaurant
25 Mar–27 Jun 11am–5:30pm
Mon, Tue, Wed, Sat, Sun
1 Jul–1 Sep 11am–5:30pm
Mon, Tue, Wed, Fri, Sat, Sun
2 Sep–29 Oct 11am–5:30pm
Mon, Tue, Wed, Sat, Sun
4 Nov–16 Dec 11am–3:30pm
Sat, Sun
6 Jan 08–24 Feb 08
11am–3:30pm Sat, Sun

House
3 Jun–27 Jun 12–5pm
Mon–Wed, Sat, Sun
1 Jul–1 Sep 12–5pm Mon, Tue,
Wed, Fri, Sat, Sun
2 Sep–29 Oct 12–5pm Mon,
Tue, Wed, Sat, Sun

Galleries only
4 Nov–16 Dec 11am–3pm Sat,
Sun
6 Jan–24 Feb 11am–3pm Sat,
Sun

Notes
Special rates and exemptions
apply for schools and
community groups

Built in 1716, this grand Georgian mansion has a dramatic exterior, and ornate Baroque interiors. The design is unusual, with a central corridor running along the whole length of the house. Outside there are interesting grounds, with a walled garden and places to picnic.

Picture perfect
In partnership with the National Gallery, Beningbrough houses over 100 famous paintings and has seven new portrait interpretation galleries. Younger visitors can also put themselves in the picture with the aid of computers, clothes and 18th-century props.

What to see
- A fully equipped Victorian laundry — how did posh people keep their clothes clean before the days of washing machines? Servants, of course!
- Discover why bedrooms were such busy places in the 18th-century.
- And what it was like to live without bathrooms.

What to do
- Let off steam in the brilliant wooden Wilderness Play area, with new 'Beningbrough Fort'.
- Explore the grounds and look for the intriguing wooden sculptures or picnic in the walled garden.
- There are seven portrait interpretation galleries, with hands-on activities including dressing up to create a computer portrait which can be emailed to yourself.

Special events
We often have family event days, including art activities, trails, theatre etc. Please contact us for details.

By the way...
- There are some cycle paths through the parkland.
- Baby-changing facilities, and we can loan you a hip-carrying infant seat.
- Wheelchairs are available and there is a lift to all floors of the house.
- Grounds have some cobbles.

Brimham Rocks

Countryside Moor

Come and scramble on these strange and fantastic rock formations, nearly 300 metres (985 ft) above the surrounding countryside — they're perfect for hide and seek and exploring. You'll often see more experienced rock climbers as well. Early Victorians believed the rocks were created by ancient Druids, but in fact the strange weathering is entirely natural.

Lovers and legends

There is a story that two young lovers leapt off a rock here because the girl's father wouldn't let them marry. As they leapt, they were miraculously saved by the wind and put down safely. It's been known as Lover's Rock ever since.

What to see

- Birds nesting in the rocks, and listen out for jackdaws.
- A long way – on a clear day the view is 64 kilometres (40 miles) across the countryside.
- If you're lucky, rabbits, grouse or even red deer.

What to do

- Look for the wishing stone with a hole in it, and put your hand in to make a wish.
- Pick bilberries in the summer.
- Count the different kinds of lichen on the rocks.

Special events

Recent events include ghostly stories and wildlife trails, as well as family walks. Give us a call to see what's on.

By the way...

- Good footwear is a must, and wrap up warm in colder weather. In July and August it is very busy here.
- Dogs have to be on a lead between April and June so that ground-nesting birds are safe.
- There's a path from the car park to the main rocks; the rest is a bit rough and has slopes.

Summerbridge, Harrogate, North Yorkshire, HG3 4DW
01423 780688

OPENING TIMES
All year 8–dusk Mon–Sun

Shop/exhibition/kiosk
17 Mar–20 May 11am–5pm Sat, Sun
21 May–30 Sep 11am–5pm Mon – Sun
6 Oct–28 Oct 11am–5pm Sat, Sun
4 Nov–16 Dec 11–dusk Sun

Notes
Coaches £12 all day

121

Cherryburn

Historic house Garden Farm River

Station Bank, Mickley,
nr Stocksfield,
Northumberland, NE43 7DD
01661 843276

OPENING TIMES

Public opening
17 Mar–28 Oct 11am–5pm
Mon, Tue, Thu, Fri, Sat, Sun

Booked groups
19 Mar–26 Oct 10am–4pm
Mon, Tue, Wed, Thu, Fri
29 Oct–29 Feb 08 10am–4pm
Mon–Sun

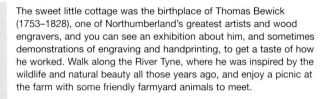

The sweet little cottage was the birthplace of Thomas Bewick (1753–1828), one of Northumberland's greatest artists and wood engravers, and you can see an exhibition about him, and sometimes demonstrations of engraving and handprinting, to get a taste of how he worked. Walk along the River Tyne, where he was inspired by the wildlife and natural beauty all those years ago, and enjoy a picnic at the farm with some friendly farmyard animals to meet.

Birdman Bewick

Thomas Bewick didn't do that well at school, and left quite early on to become apprentice to an engraver, helping to engrave the designs on banknotes. But his real love was birds and wildlife, and one of his most famous books of engravings was the *Birds of Britain*. He'd have been pleased to know that the beautiful Bewick's Swan was named in his memory.

What to see
- Some of Bewick's engravings, cut into wood – nowadays we can just take a photo instead!
- Demonstrations of hand printing and engraving.
- A secret garden.
- Chickens, rabbits, lambs and donkeys, who live around the cobbled farmyard.

What to do
- Bring a picnic and enjoy it in the garden (we don't have a café, but we sell lovely cakes, snacks, tea, coffee and soft drinks).
- Pick up some prints made from Bewick's original engravings at the shop.
- Take a stroll along the beautiful River Tyne.

Special events
Recently we've had folk music and country dance in the farmyard, drawing workshops, and engraving demonstrations. Usually the cost is included in admission, and there's something going on most Sunday afternoons.

By the way...
- If you contact us in advance, we can provide touchable objects and help to make your visit more accessible. There are some steps to get in and out of the building, and the farmyard is cobbled.
- We can provide a braille guide, and there's an adapted WC.

East Riddlesden Hall

Historic house Garden Maze Pond

This intimate 17th-century manor house is in the heart of Brontë country. Back in the 1600s, it was one of 19 (count 'em!) houses owned by wealthy royalist James Murgatroyd – an entrepreneur, who was also involved in coal mining, cloth manufacture and farming. He remodelled the house with flamboyant gothic architecture and some ornate plasterwork ceilings. In the summer, guides in authentic costume will help you to feel that you've gone back in time.

That's one hefty heifer

The Airedale Heifer, depicted in an 1830 painting at Riddlesden, was a legendary creature in nearby Keighley. It was supposedly 3.3 metres (11 feet) long and weighed more than one and a quarter tons. People used to come from miles around to see it.

What to see

- A room with a bricked-in window so that ladies didn't have to look at the outside loo!
- A 17th-century kitchen, with no mod cons.
- Intricate tapestries and embroideries that would have taken hours to make...
- ... which accounts for the big fireplaces and cosy wood paneling.
- An enormous 17th-century oak-framed barn.

What to do

- Visit the Airedale Heifer playground and grass maze, with swings, slides and animal rockers.
- Chat to the ducks on the pond.

Special events

Get in touch to see what we have on. We have spooky Halloween activities and Christmas Carol concerts, and Easter activities for children.

By the way...

- We have a handling collection of 17th-century items, and there are scented plants in the garden, as well as a braille guide.
- There are some steps, but the ground floor is accessible, and we have wheelchairs. The grounds are fully accessible and we have portable ramps. There are quite a few steps to the café.

Bradford Road, Keighley, West Yorkshire, BD20 5EL
01535 607075

OPENING TIMES

House
17 Mar–4 Nov 12–5pm Tue, Wed, Sat, Sun

Shop/tea-room
17 Mar–4 Nov 12–5pm Tue, Wed, Sat, Sun
10 Nov–16 Dec 12–4pm Sat, Sun

Notes
£1 off admission when arriving via Keighley & District Transport buses

North East

Fountains Abbey & Studley Royal

Historic house Water garden Mill Garden Park Abbey ruins

Fountains, Ripon,
North Yorkshire, HG4 3DY
01765 608888

OPENING TIMES

**Abbey/garden/visitor
centre/shop/restaurant***
1 Mar–31 Oct 10am–5pm
Mon–Sun
1 Nov–28 Feb 08 10am–4pm
Mon, Tue, Wed, Thu, Sat, Sun

Deer park
All year Dawn–dusk Mon–Sun

St Mary's
1 Apr–30 Sep 12–4pm
Mon–Sun

Mill
1 Mar–31 Oct 10am–5pm
Mon–Sun
1 Nov–28 Feb 08 10am–4pm
Mon, Tue, Wed, Thu, Sat, Sun

Notes
Groups (31+) £6, children £3.
EH members free. Visitor
centre, deer park, St Mary's
Church: free

There's so much atmosphere to soak up at this fascinating World
Heritage Site. Explore the spectacular ruins of a Cistercian abbey
and watermill, founded in 1132 by 13 Benedictine monks who were
after a simpler life. You can also visit rooms in Fountains Hall, an
Elizabethan mansion, and enjoy the Georgian water garden – one of
the best surviving examples, complete with lakes, cascades and
temples. There's a cute litte church and, last but not least, the
medieval deer park is home to around 500 deer and other wildlife.

Woolly wealth

The monks were so busy praying that all the day-to-day labour was
done by ordinary 'lay' folk. But they were quite a canny lot – the
monastery was in the wool business, with sheep nibbling the rich
grasslands for miles around, and the monks had quite an economic
empire.

What to see

- Dramatic abbey ruins with Gothic arches towering above you.
- The trough where the monks washed their feet – they had baths
  only four times a year!
- Ducks and swans paddling by the statues in the water garden.
- If you're lucky, a bat whizzing by your ear.

- Spot the different temples, statues and other strange little buildings – called follies – in the gardens.
- Explore the garden and find the Serpentine Tunnel, the Grotto and the Half Moon Pond.
- Walk up to Anne Boleyn's seat, a folly with a wonderful 'Surprise' view.
- Have a go at the quiz and trail, and see if you can identify the different kinds of deer.

Special events

In the holidays we have children's trails and craft workshops, and family tours of the Abbey, when you can dress up in monks' robes and learn more about their daily life. We occasionally have free floodlit drives through the estate for less able visitors.

By the way...

- The water gardens offer interesting sounds, and we also have a model of the Abbey in the visitor centre, and a braille guide.
- Some areas of the grounds are less accessible, but we have maps of level routes and you can book a PMV vehicle.
- There are wheelchairs available, but you need to book. There are steps (with handrails) at Fountains Hall.

Gibside

Park Countryside River Wood

nr Rowlands Gill, Burnopfield,
Newcastle upon Tyne,
Tyne & Wear, NE16 6BG
01207 541820

OPENING TIMES

Grounds
5 Mar–28 Oct 10am–6pm
Mon–Sun
29 Oct–29 Feb 08 10am–4pm
Mon–Sun

Chapel
19 Mar–28 Oct 11am–4:30pm
Mon–Sun

Stables
5 Mar–28 Oct 11am–4:30pm
Mon–Sun
29 Oct–29 Feb 08
11am–3:30pm Mon–Sun

Shop/tea-room
5 Mar–28 Oct 11am–5pm Mon
–Sun
29 Oct–29 Feb 08 11am–4pm
Mon–Sun

One of the North's finest landscapes, the 18th-century estate is the former home of the Queen Mother's family, the Bowes-Lyons. There are many miles of walks through woodland and by the River Derwent. Some quirky buildings, including the Column of Liberty and a Palladian chapel. Streams to paddle in, woods to explore and open spaces to run around or play a game of footie in.

We're proud of our conveniences!

We just can't hold it in – we have to tell you that our loos were judged the best in Britain by the British Toilet Association (really!) a few years ago. So, come and try out the thrones in the Queen Mum's old garden.

What to see

- The estate is a Site of Special Scientific Interest – look out for red squirrels, kingfishers and other wildlife.
- Not to mention hundreds of scampering rabbits.
- The Liberty Column – built after the 1745 Jacobite Rebellion and taller than Nelson's.

What to do

- Explore over 25 kilometres (16 miles) of woodland and riverside walks. Not all at once – pick up leaflets of routes in the info centre.
- See the restored stables – not only an education centre but also still used for real horses.
- Bring the dog – the grounds are a good place for walking – but on the lead, please.

Special events

Check to see if we're having any children's days coming up. At no extra charge, they include magicians, races and more.

By the way...

- Some of the buildings are being restored, but there's still a lot to see.
- There are baby-changing facilities and a children's menu in the tea-room.
- The grounds have some steep slopes, but there's a map of an accessible route.

Hadrian's Wall & Housestead's Fort

Countryside Museum

A wild and evocative World Heritage Site offering a taste of the Roman soldier's life – communal loos and all. The Wall was built around AD 122, when the Roman Empire was at its height, and even now the ruins are impressive, and looking after the Wall is a full-time job. Housesteads Fort is one of the best-preserved of the sixteen forts along the Wall.

It's cold up north

Soldiers from sunnier climes were brought in to guard the Wall – the Roman name for Housesteads was *Vercovicium*, which means 'effective fighters'. But some of those foreign soldiers were pretty miserable up on their cold lookout posts – and you might want to bring a sweater, too.

What to see

- Ruins of Roman granaries, barracks, a hospital and some of the first flushing toilets.
- A model of the fort as it would have been.
- Wonderful views across the countryside.

Bardon Mill, Hexham,
Northumberland, NE47 6NN
01434 344363

OPENING TIMES
1 Apr–30 Sep 10am–6pm Mon –Sun
1 Oct–29 Feb 08 10am–4pm Mon–Sun

Notes
Free to NT and EH members. Hadrian's Wall, NT information centre and shop free

What to do

- Walk like a Roman... march alongside the Wall, repelling imaginary Picts and Scots.
- If it's a bit chilly, grab a drink and a sandwich at the kiosk, and sit inside to warm up.
- Have a look in the museum, to find out more on the history of the Wall.

By the way...

- The paths are a bit uneven at Housesteads and on the Wall. But there's a ramped access to the Wall at Steel Rigg.
- You can drive right up to the museum.
- Please keep your dog on a lead because there are sheep and ground-nesting birds nearby.

Hardcastle Crags

Mill Countryside Wood

This beautiful woodland valley is tranquil and unspoilt. Come on foot if you can – the parking area gets very busy – and potter about near the trickling streams, or listen out for the drumming of woodpeckers

ANTastic
The Crags are home to the northern hairy wood ant – they don't sting, but do look a bit fearsome with their mini-pincers and have a habit of spraying you with formic acid if they get cross. So, don't get too close – and don't ask them to shave their legs!

What to see
- Deep rocky ravines, tumbling streams and the millstone grit Crags.
- Huge anthills, made by our hairy ant-y friends.
- Gibson Mill – an 18th-century cotton mill that's being restored.

What to do
- Try one of our way-marked walks, the easier 'Slurring Rock Saunter' or the more energetic 'Crags Constitutional'.
- Or try our special sensory trail, with clues as to what's good to touch, smell or listen to, as well as look at.
- Let your dog enjoy a scramble, too.

Special events
You can book a guided walk or a special orienteering course, and there's a BSL Interpreter at all our programmed events. We've had prehistoric survival days for older kids, and bat walks and dawn chorus. Give us a call.

By the way...
- Parking is limited and there is congestion during busy times. Come by bus!
- Disabled parking is possible, but ask if you want to park at Gibson Mill.
- Picnicking is possible.

Estate Office, Hollin Hall,
Crimsworth Dean,
Hebden Bridge,
West Yorkshire, HX7 7AP
01422 844518

OPENING TIMES
Hardcastle Crags
All year Mon–Sun

Gibson Mill
1 Mar–30 Sep 11am–4:30pm
Sat, Sun
1 Oct–28 Feb 08
11am–3:30pm Sat, Sun

Muddy Boots Café
1 Mar–18 Apr 11am–4:30pm
Sat, Sun
18 Apr–30 Sep 11am–4:30pm
Tue, Wed, Thu, Sat, Sun
1 Oct–28 Feb 08
11am–3:30pm Sat, Sun

Nostell Priory

Historic house Garden

Doncaster Road,
Nostell, nr Wakefield,
West Yorkshire, WF4 1QE
01924 863892

OPENING TIMES

House
17 Mar–4 Nov 1pm–5pm Wed,
Thu, Fri, Sat, Sun
7 Dec–16 Dec 12–4pm Mon
–Sun

Grounds/shop/tea-room
17 Mar–4 Nov 11am–5:30pm
Wed, Thu, Fri, Sat, Sun
10 Nov–2 Dec 11am–4:30pm
Sat, Sun
7 Dec–16 Dec 11am–4:30pm
Mon–Sun

Park
All year 9am–5pm Mon–Sun

Plenty for the family to do in the landscaped grounds of this magnificent 18th-century house, built on the site of an original medieval priory in 1733. There are paintings by Breughel and Holbein, and probably the finest collection of Chippendale furniture in the world. It's like a really good episode of Antiques Roadshow!

A world in miniature

Peek inside the magical 18th-century dolls' house, which is 2 metres (6 feet) high. There's a mini-leather dog, an ivory mouse, and a dining table all laid out with tiny cutlery and silver plates. Try and spot the difference in the way the figures of the family and the servants were made.

What to see

- Pets' graves in the rose garden and cows in the park
- Child-sized Chippendale chairs — sorry, you can't sit on them!
- A clock made by John Harrison, with workings inside made of wood.

What to do

- In the gardens, find the Obelisk Lodge in the shape of a pyramid.
- Burn off some energy in the adventure playground, or watch the kids doing that from the tea-room.
- Walk around the lake and say hello to the ducks.

Special events

We have family croquet and and a giant chess set in the garden plus spooky Halloween evenings. Get in touch to see what's on.

By the way...

- With advance notice, we can provide a lot of touchable objects and surfaces.
- Wheelchairs can be booked; a lift is available to upper floors.
- There are baby-changing and feeding facilities, and we can loan you baby slings and infant-carriers (sorry, no pushchairs allowed in the house).

Nunnington Hall

Historic house Garden

This 17th-century stone house on the banks of the River Rye has some fascinating surprises. Creep up one of the three staircases to the nursery and the haunted room. And in the attics you'll discover the Carlisle collection of miniature rooms – with everything from titchy musical instruments to minuscule files and sandpaper in the carpenter's shop.

Spooky story
People say that the panelled bedroom is haunted by a spooky lady ghost who can fly through the 400-year old wooden walls.

What to see
- That amazing collection of tiny objects and houses.
- Needlework samplers made by young girls in the 19th century.
- Watch out for the ghost!

What to do
- Find out why the tea caddy in the drawing room has a lock on it.
- Look out for the stuffed animal heads and skins collected on expeditions to India and Africa.
- Watch the peacocks strut their stuff in the riverside walled garden.

Special events
Events all season, including children's trails during school holidays.

By the way...
- There are picnic tables in the tea garden, as well as a children's menu.
- We can loan you infant seats and toddler reins, and there are baby-changing facilities.
- It's fairly accessible, and we have wheelchairs and can provide assistance. Dogs in the car park only, please, but we have shaded parking.

Nunnington, nr York,
North Yorkshire, YO62 5UY
01439 748283

OPENING TIMES
17 Mar–31 May 12–5pm Wed, Thu, Fri, Sat, Sun
1 Jun–31 Aug 12–5:30pm Wed, Thu, Fri, Sat, Sun
1 Sep–4 Nov 12–5pm Tue, Wed, Thu, Fri, Sat, Sun

North East

QUEEN ANNE DRAWING ROOM

131

Souter Lighthouse

Coastline Nature reserve Museum Historic building

North East

Coast Road, Whitburn,
Sunderland,
Tyne & Wear SR6 7NH
0191 529 3161

OPENING TIMES
17 Mar–28 Oct 11am–5pm
Mon, Tue, Wed, Thu, Sat, Sun

Notes
Entry to shop and tea-room free

Souter Lighthouse, with its jaunty red and white stripes, is an exciting place to head for if you're in the area. So long as they are accompanied by adults, children can make it up the lighthouse tower's spiral staircase.

All lit up
Souter Lighthouse was opened in 1871 after dozens of ships had foundered on submerged rocks along this dangerous stretch of coast – it was the first lighthouse to be powered by electricity.

What to see
- Victorian machines in the engine room, the heart of the lighthouse.
- At the top of the tower you can look out to sea for miles. Don't get too puffed out – there are 76 steps!
- Watch a 9-minute video about the lighthouse.

What to do
- Explore a replica of the cottage where the first keeper Henry Millet lived c.1900 with his family.
- Send a message in Morse code on the signaller, and decode signalling flags using CCTV.
- Have a picnic and a bracing walk along the clifftop footpath above Marsden Bay, where you can look down on the swooping seabirds!

Special events
Annual nature-themed festival in July.

By the way...
- Although access for pushchairs and those with restricted mobility is limited, a camera at the top of the lighthouse tower can be operated from the ground floor, so everyone can enjoy the view from the top!

Treasurer's House

Historic house Garden

Children will be fascinated to spot the fussy habits of the man who lived in this elegant house at the beginning of the 20th century. Can you believe that Frank Green had studs set into the floor to tell servants where to put the furniture?! And there are bossy signs all over the place... How many can you find? The house is set in the tranquil Minster Close – great for a rainy day.

Spooky story
A plumber was working in the cellar in the 1950s when he heard a trumpet and saw Roman soldiers coming out of the wall. He was so shocked he fell off his ladder! What's amazing is that the soldiers seemed to have no feet – archaeologists have now found that the Roman road which went though the house was 45 cm (18 inches) lower than the new floor. Weird...

What to see
- A model ship made out of bones (left over from meal times!).
- Some really clever paint techniques, of pretend wood and carving.
- Look out for Frisk, Mr Green's favourite dog.

What to do
- Find out how they stopped mice climbing up the table legs.
- See how fast your eyes can adapt to the darkness in the King's Room, kept that way to preserve the fabrics.

Minster Yard, York,
North Yorkshire YO1 7JL.
01904 624247

OPENING TIMES
17 Mar–4 Nov 11am–4:30pm
Mon, Tue, Wed, Thu, Sat, Sun
5 Nov–30 Nov 11am–3pm
Mon, Tue, Wed, Thu, Sat, Sun

Notes
Large groups welcome but need to divide so not more than 15 touring the house at a time. Charges apply to NT members

North East

Wallington

Historic house Garden Park Countryside Lake Wood

Cambo, Morpeth,
Northumberland, NE61 4AR
01670 773600

OPENING TIMES

House
17 Mar–2 Sep 1pm–5:30pm
Mon, Wed, Thu, Fri, Sat, Sun
3 Sep–4 Nov 1pm–4:30pm
Mon, Wed, Thu, Fri, Sat, Sun

Walled garden
1 Apr–30 Sep 10am–7pm Mon
–Sun
1 Oct–31 Oct 10am–6pm Mon
–Sun
1 Nov–29 Feb 08 10am–4pm
Mon – Sun

Shop/restaurant
1 Mar–25 May
10:30am–5:30pm Mon, Wed,
Thu, Fri, Sat, Sun
26 May–2 Sep
10:30am–5:30pm Mon – Sun
3 Sep–4 Nov 10:30am–4:30pm
Mon, Wed, Thu, Fri, Sat, Sun
5 Nov–15 Feb 08
10:30am–4:30pm Wed, Thu,
Fri, Sat, Sun
16 Feb 08–28 Feb 08
10:30am–5:30pm Mon, Wed,
Thu, Fri, Sat, Sun

Farm shop
17 Mar–31 Oct 10:30am–5pm
Mon–Sun

Don't be fooled by the plain exterior of this 17th-century house,
home to many generations of the Blackett and Trevelyan families.
Inside there's oodles of fancy plasterwork, gorgeous Pre-Raphaelite
paintings and many fascinating objects. Outside there's a fabulous
garden with sculptures, water features and even a wildlife hide.

The mole's revenge

Did you know that King William III died when his horse tripped over a
mole hill? The horse had previously belonged to Sir John Fenwick, who
owned Wallington and whose estates were forfeit to the Crown upon
his execution for treason. Jacobite supporters – enemies of William –
used to drink a toast to the mole, or 'the little black velvet gentleman',
for this sweet justice!

What to see

- A stuffed porcupine fish and other oddities in the Cabinet of
  Curiosities, brought to Wallington by Maria, the wife of the 5th Baronet.
- A collection of dolls' houses in the servants' quarters. Peep through
  two keyholes and a mouse hole to see the mouse house.
- Some very large stone Griffin heads on the lawn – like
  something out of *Harry Potter*!

What to do
- Visit the children's room (no adults allowed!) filled with old-fashioned games and toys.
- Imagine doing loads of washing-up in that kitchen without a dishwasher!
- Have a clamber around in the adventure playground.

Special events
We have a range of events for all the family – Easter trails, Mayday celebrations, a Family Fun Day and lots more. Get in touch!

By the way...
- There are lots of small objects within the house, so we do encourage babies to enjoy visiting from the comfort of a front-carrying sling, which we're happy to loan around the house.
- The courtyard is a nice place for picnics, and there's a children's menu in the restaurant.

COASTING ALONG

The National Trust owns over 700 miles of coastline, ranging from windswept cliffs to sumptuous sandy beaches. We'll let this sample selection entice you – visit our web page for full details on all our wonderful coastal sites!

If it's a traditional day at the beach you're after, **Studland Beach & Nature Reserve**, in Dorset, has 5 kilometres (3 miles) of sandy beaches, and safe shallow water to swim in. While you're there, take a walk along the Jurassic Coast, to **Old Harry Rocks**.

In Wales, the 8 kilometres (5 miles) of superb beach at **Rhossili Bay**, at the tip of the Gower Peninsula is the place to head for if you've got young children. While you're there, take a breezy cliff walk, or look out for the wooden ribs of the shipwrecked *Helvetia* at low tide. The **Lleyn Peninsula**, Pembrokeshire and **Cardigan Bay** are also wonderful Welsh coastal sites, offering dramatic cliffs, beaches and a chance to see rare birds and other wildlife.

Cornwall has some of the most stunning coastal scenery in the UK, with secluded coves, craggy cliffs and sandy beaches. **Crackington Haven** is a perfect family beach, with surfer's waves and rock pools as well as plenty of sand at low tide. It's not itself an NT site, but the cliff walks either side are, including 'High Cliff', the highest cliff in Cornwall. **Boscastle**, on the North coast, is a dramatic starting point for a coastal walk (a bit of a tough one, so maybe not for the youngest members of the family), and **Fowey** and **Kynance Cove** and **Lizard Point** are both excellent places for a day's outing with some walking and views attached. Cornwall offers a great many gorgeous cliff walks (but do keep dogs on the lead and kids away from the edge!).

The North Norfolk Coast is a bird-watcher's paradise. Enjoy the boat trip out to **Blakeney Point**, where you can get close to basking seals. Walk across the marches at **Morston** and **Stiffkey**, or drink in the view of the sea from **Sheringham Park**, which also has some great walks and an old steam railway. Romp around at **West Runton** or Brancaster – with a trip to **Scolt Head Island** if the tides permit.

Irish coast-lovers also have a wealth of choices. Marvel at the **Giant's Causeway**, and then take a giant walk down 22.5 kilometres (14 miles) of the **North Antrim Cliff** path (or just a little walk down a bit of it!). **Portstewart Strand** – a magnificent 3-kilometre (2-mile) strand from Portstewart to the Bann estuary – is also a great place to watch birds feeding and stretch your legs.

If you fancy a boat trip, there are exciting coastal sites at the **Farne Islands**, **Brownsea Island** and **Lundy**, to name a few. But make sure you call first to see if the boats are running – it sometimes depends on the tides or weather. Or how about a wobbly walk across a rope bridge to **Carrick-a-Rede**, a rocky island in Country Antrim!

Lighthouses

There are hundreds of National Trust-owned buildings on the coast, including radar stations, roman forts and coastguard cottages. And the many lighthouses are particularly good to explore. How about **Souter Lighthouse**, in Tyne & Wear, the world's first electric lighthouse? You can take a cliff-top walk to it, and climb up to look at the fantastic views over Marsden Bay.

And if lighthouses grab you, here's a few more you can try! There's **Longstore Lighthouse**, **Orford Ness**, **Beachy Head** and the **Gribbin**, for starters. And there are more at **South Foreland**, near Dover, on the **Lizard Peninsula**, on **Lundy** island and – perhaps the oldest one of all – a medieval lighthouse at **St Catherine's Oratory**, on the Isle of Wight. Check our web pages for much more on maritime buildings you can visit.

So get out to the coast and feel the wind in your hair, it's an exhilarating way for all the family to get some exercise and enjoy the beauty of the natural environment. Visit the National Trust website at **www.nationaltrust.org.uk** to find more information on all the other coastal sites that you can explore, and to download maps of coastal walks.

Chirk Castle

Fortress   Garden   Parkland

Chirk,
Wrexham, LL14 5AF
01691 777701

OPENING TIMES

Castle
24 Mar–30 Jun 12–5pm Wed,
Thu, Fri, Sat, Sun
1 Jul–31 Aug 12–5pm Tue, Wed,
Thu, Fri, Sat, Sun
1 Sep–30 Sep 12–5pm Wed,
Thu, Fri, Sat, Sun
1 Oct–4 Nov 12–4pm Wed, Thu,
Fri, Sat, Sun

Garden & estate
As castle 10am–6pm

NT shop
As castle 11am–5pm

Tea-room/resturant
As castle 10am–5pm

Chirk Castle was built in the late 13th century and is a rather tough-looking character, with towers and thick brick walls, and a top-of-the-range dungeon on two levels. The castle stands on a hilltop looking over the Ceiriog valley to the south, so nobody can creep up on it unawares. The interior has been refurbished and added to over the years, and it's still home to the Myddleton family, whose ancestor Sir Thomas bought it in 1595 for 5000 pounds.

Bloody hand!
Legend has it that the red hand in the family coat-of-arms comes from a rather macabre running race. Two of the Myddleton lads argued over who should inherit, and agreed to settle the dispute by racing to the castle gates. But the first boy was just reaching out to touch the gates when the other one reached out with his sword and cut off his hand. Now is that called cheating or 'winning on a technicality'?

What to see
- The rather grim dungeons with their very tiny windows. Don't get shut in!
- The 'murder holes' in the stairs in Adam's towers – soldiers threw hot oil and stones down them to hit the enemy below.
- Genuine suits of armour from the Civil War.
- The huge elaborate iron gates – look for the eagles' heads and the Myddleton family crest.

What to do
- Put the kids in the stocks (but please, do remember to take them home afterwards).
- Try on historic costumes and lay siege to the castle in the family-activity room.
- Have fun on the hanging ropes, tyres and wooden logs in the children's adventure playground.
- Borrow outdoor Tracker Packs to explore the countryside.

Special events
We have family-activity Thursdays throughout summer school holidays from costumes and armour to plagues and potions. Special Easter trails and Haunted Happenings, Medieval festivals and living history re-enactments.

By the way...
- There are picnic tables by the play area and a rustic picnic area by the carpark.
- Children's quizzes for castle and garden always available.
- There are quite a few steps through the castle and spiral stone staircases in the tower and down to the dungeon.

Dinefwr Park and Castle

Castle Historic house Park

Wales & Northern Ireland

Llandeilo,
Carmarthenshire, SA19 6RT
01558 824512

OPENING TIMES
17 Mar–28 Oct 11am–5pm
Mon, Thu, Fri, Sat, Sun

Dinefwr is a beautiful 18th-century park enclosing a medieval deer park. Come into the house, too, built in 1660 but now with a Victorian façade. Our friendly volunteers will be glad to tell you more, and little fingers are allowed to touch many of the objects. There are footpaths in the park, leading to the castle, bog wood and some outstanding views of the Towy Valley.

The Romans woz 'ere
Recent geophysical surveys show that there are not one but two big Roman forts hidden under the ground in Dinefwr Park. It could be the largest Roman garrison fort in Wales. Excavations began in June 2005 to find out just what's down there.

What to see
- Shy fallow deer munching away under the trees.
- A herd of rare Dinefwr White Park cattle. They're very... white.
- A beautiful fancy ceiling in the house.

What to do
- Try out the children's house quiz; we'll help out if you get stuck!
- Enjoy a scenic walk: take the pushchair along our boardwalk through Bog Wood to the mill pond (see how many dragonflies you can spot there).

Special events
We often host family-friendly events. Recently we've had badger-watching and displays of vintage machines and classic cars. Give us a call to see what's on.

By the way...
- Dogs are allowed in the outer park only, on a lead.
- We have baby-changing and feeding facilities and a children's menu in the tea-room (not NT).
- You can book a wheelchair, and there's also a virtual tour of the house.

Dolaucothi Gold Mines
Countryside Museum Mines

Come for a guided tour of the unique underground workings which have great archeological importance. And have a go at gold-panning. If you find any, it's yours. There's also an interesting new exhibition on mining history and working trains on the mine floor.

There's gold in them thar hills
... well, not much now, although the mines were in use from Roman times 2000 years ago, right up the 20th century. The Romans built a fort at Pumsaint, so they could keep an eye on things, and brought in slaves and local people to do the digging for them.

What to see
- Tunnels, pits, channels, tanks – basically, if you can dig one, it's probably here.
- A collection of 1930s mining machinery in the main mine yard.
- Pick marks in the rocks made by Roman slaves.

What to do
- Try gold-panning, and you'll realise just how frustrating looking for gold can be.
- Go for a walk in the wooded hills, or hire a cycle at the nearby Information Centre in Pumsaint.
- Experience what mining would have been like on the hour-long tour with only lamps to light your way (younger children allowed only at the discretion of staff – telephone to ask).

Special events
We have an annual living history weekend when we all go back to Roman times, and have visiting crafts people and sometimes Roman cookery. You can come and join in – contact us to find out this year's date.

By the way...
- We have a new level tour of the mine yard suitable for the less mobile.
- Good idea to wear good shoes for the underground tours; it can be a bit slippy down there.
- There's a caravan site and also fishing available on the estate.

Pumsaint, Llanwrda,
Carmarthenshire, SA19 8RR
01558 650177

OPENING TIMES
Mines
25 Mar–29 Oct 10am–5pm
Mon–Sun

Shop
25 Mar–29 Oct 10am–5pm
Mon–Sun

Christmas shop
8 Nov–17 Dec 11am–4pm
Wed, Thu, Fri, Sat, Sun

Tea-room
25 Mar–29 Oct 10am–5pm
Mon–Sun

Erddig

Historic house Garden Park Countryside Wood

Wrexham, LL13 0YT
01978 355314

OPENING TIMES

House
25 Mar–12 Apr 12–4pm Mon,
Tue, Wed, Sat, Sun
15 Apr–28 Jun 12–5pm Mon,
Tue, Wed, Sat, Sun
1 Jul–31 Aug 12–5pm Mon,
Tue, Wed, Thu, Sat, Sun
2 Sep–30 Sep 12–5pm Mon,
Tue, Wed, Sat, Sun
1 Oct–29 Oct 12–4pm Mon,
Tue, Wed, Sat, Sun

Garden
25 Mar–28 Jun 11am–6pm
Mon, Tue, Wed, Sat, Sun
1 Jul–31 Aug 10am–6pm Mon,
Tue, Wed, Thu, Sat, Sun
2 Sep–30 Sep 11am–6pm
Mon, Tue, Wed, Sat, Sun
1 Oct–29 Oct 11am–5pm Mon,
Tue, Wed, Sat, Sun
4 Nov–17 Dec 11am–4pm Sat,
Sun

Restaurant/shop/plants
25 Mar–28 Jun 11am–5:15pm
Mon, Tue, Wed, Sat, Sun

The original house was finished in 1687 and was added to over the years as the home of the Yorke family. They were a rather eccentric bunch and chose not to install electricity, gas or mains water until well into the 20th century. Don't be fooled by the plain brickwork exterior: inside, the lavish furnishings are outstanding and the servants' rooms give an intriguing taste of life 'below stairs'.

Family values
The Yorkes all shared an interest in antiquity and hoarding things, no matter how trivial. Many of them were vegetarians – in 1749 at age five, Philip Yorke apparently 'chused chiefly to dine on vegetables'. They were extremely fond of all their servants, and even commissioned portraits of them all – complete with little verses penned by the family.

What to see
- A grand kitchen – detached from the house to reduce the risk of fire. And many original objects in the stables, forge and more.
- An 18th-century waterfall known as the 'cup and saucer' in the park.
- Very special Chinese wallpaper in the house.

What to do

- Look for the gamekeeper, the housemaid and the blacksmith among the portraits of the servants in the servants' hall and basement passage.
- Visit the walled garden to spot rare varieties of fruit – did you know there was an apple called an Edlesborsdorfer? Neither did we!
- Take a horse-drawn carriage ride.

Special events

We have authentic demonstrations of restored historic equipment, and sometimes you'll meet some 'Victorian' servants in the house. We also have special days, from our increasingly popular Apple Festival to craft making. Call us to find out what holiday activities are planned.

By the way...

- We have wheelchairs, and a ramped entrance, but there are stairs in the house.
- Most rooms have no electric light – avoid dull days if you want a really close look at the pictures.
- There are three different walks to follow in the grounds, but please keep your dog on the lead.

Llanerchaeron

Historic house Garden Park Farm

Ciliau Aeron, nr Aberaeron,
Ceredigion SA48 8DG
01545 570200

OPENING TIMES

House
25 Mar–23 Jul
11:30am–4:30pm Wed, Thu,
Fri, Sat, Sun
24 Jul–3 Sep 11:30am–4:30pm
Tue, Wed, Thu, Fri, Sat, Sun
4 Sep–29 Oct
11:30am–4:30pm Wed, Thu,
Fri, Sat, Sun

Farm/garden
25 Mar–23 Jul 11am–5pm
Wed, Thu, Fri, Sat, Sun
24 Jul–3 Sep 11am–5pm Tue,
Wed, Thu, Fri, Sat, Sun
4 Sep–29 Oct 11am–5pm Wed,
Thu, Fri, Sat, Sun

Set in the beautiful Dyffryn Aeron, the estate survived virtually unaltered into the 20th century.

Do it yourself
No trips to the supermarket here, everything consumed or used on the property was produced here – the house is a great example of self-sufficiency. The workers would have produced all their own cheese and milk in the dairy, they'd have salted their own meats for preservation and even brewed their own beer!

What to see
- Visit the dairy, laundry, brewery and salting house and learn how they would have made everything themselves.
- The restored walled gardens full of home-grown fruit, vegetables and herbs.
- Traditional farming activities in progress: lambing, shearing and hay-making.

What to do
- Home Farm is a working organic farm, so there's loads to learn about; take a guided tour and then visit the Education Centre.
- Enjoy one of the many walks around the estate and parkland.
- Learn about the breeds of animals, including Welsh Black cattle, Llanwenog sheep and rare Welsh pigs.

By the way...
- Parents can take part in adult study days.

Penrhyn Castle

Historic house Garden Museum Wood

Penrhyn looks like a fairytale medieval castle, but actually it was built in the 19th century. So, who cares if it's a fake – it's well worth a visit because it's packed with goodies, like the doll's museum and railway museum, and has a wonderful adventure playground, too.

Easy as A B C
Richard Pennant, who lived here, made a fortune from the local slate quarry. Every year his workers made 136,000 slates for children to write on in school. Wonder if the children were grateful!

What to see
- An industrial railway museum in the stable block, and a model railway museum.
- A large collection of 19th- and 20th-century dolls.
- And can you spot two chamber pots in the dining room? They were there so the men didn't have to leave to go to the loo after dinner – yuck!

What to do
- Visit the Victorian servants' quarters, set up to show the preparations for the banquet put on for the Prince of Wales in 1894. They had pineapple ice cream and foie gras in aspic. Very tasty.
- Look at the one-ton slate bed made for Queen Victoria. Sounds pretty uncomfortable.
- Explore the formal Victorian walled garden and the adventure playground.

Bangor,
Gwynedd, LL57 4HN.
01248 353084

OPENING TIMES
Castle/grounds/tea-room/shop/museums
31 Mar–4 Nov 11am–5pm
Mon, Wed, Thu, Fri, Sat, Sun

Wales & Northern Ireland

continued…

Special events

We have quite a few family events and activities. Recently we've had Knights and Castles Fun Day, archery and hands-on cooking activities. Call us to find out what's planned.

By the way...

- Baby-changing and feeding facilities, plus sling loan (sorry, no pushchairs in the house). Children's guide and quiz/trail and also a children's menu.
- Touchable objects, including engines in the Railway Museum.
- We can lend you a wheelchair, and the entrance is ramped. There are stairs to the upper floors.

Plas Newydd

Historic house Garden Park Coastline Museum Boat trip

A very grand ivy-covered mansion, Plas Newydd simply means 'new place' in Welsh. It was built in the 18th century, and is still home to the Marquess of Anglesey. There's a big collection of paintings by Rex Whistler and a Military museum with interesting artifacts. It is set in large gardens, with a marine walk along the Menai Straits and spectacular views of Snowdonia.

Little and large!
See Rex Whistler's illustrations for *Gulliver's Travels*, costume and stage designs and caricatures. Gaze out over the Menai Strait, with views to Snowdonia and Robert Stephenson's Britannia Bridge.

Llanfairpwll,
Anglesey, LL61 6DQ
01248 714795

OPENING TIMES
House
31 Mar–31 Oct 12–5pm Mon, Tue, Wed, Sat, Sun
Garden/walks
31 Mar–31 Oct 11am–5:30pm Mon, Tue, Wed, Sat, Sun

Shop/tea-room
31 Mar–31 Oct
10:30am–5:30pm Mon, Tue, Wed, Sat, Sun
3 Nov–16 Dec 11am–4pm Sat, Sun

continued…

147

What to see
- An enormous painting by Rex Whistler – can you find Neptune's footsteps?
- An artificial leg made for the 1st Marquess of Anglesey. The Marquess' father carelessly lost the real one in the Battle of Waterloo.

What to do
- Clamber in the tree house, built for the Marquess' kids.
- For an additional charge, you can take an historical boat trip that departs from by the house; it takes around 40 minutes.

Special events
We've had spooky Halloween fun days and circus workshops in the past. Contact us to see what's on.

By the way...
- It's licensed for civil wedding ceremonies, wedding receptions and formal dinners, so if you'd like a nice Plas to get hitched in...
- Family friendly with baby-changing facilities and baby slings for loan, as well as a children's play area.
- Lower floors accessible, and there are wheelchairs available.

Powis Castle & Garden

Castle Garden Museum

If you like the idea of a dramatic medieval castle rising over world-famous gardens with statues and even an orangery, Powis is for you. The castle was originally built around 1200, as a fortress for the Welsh Princes of Powys. Over the years the Herbert family have packed it with paintings, sculptures and a fascinating collection of treasures from India, displayed in the Clive Museum.

What's in a name, Clive?

Edward Clive (1785–1848) inherited Powis from his mother's side of the family, but only if he agreed to change his name to Herbert. Things didn't end so well – he was shot to death by one of his own sons in a tragic accident. This son was apparently known to other members of the family ever after as 'Bag Dad' – not in the best of taste!

What to see

- A solid gold tiger head encrusted with precious stones and 300-year-old giant yew hedges – imagine clipping those without electric clippers.
- The igloo shaped ice house – used to store ice before fridges came along.

What to do

- Have a go at the children's quiz.
- Find a giant stone foot sculpture in the Wilderness Garden.
- Run up and down the steep garden terraces.

Special events

Our intrepid hedging team explains how they look after those yews, and at other times you can have a behind-the-scenes look at the private rooms and museum. There are some holiday activities and an annual Easter Egg hunt. Get in touch for more information.

By the way...

- Powis is very popular and we sometimes have timed tickets at busy periods.
- Because of the steep gardens and steps some parts of the property are not very accessible to people in wheelchairs.

Welshpool,
Powys, SY21 8RF
01938 551929

OPENING TIMES

Garden
17 Mar–31 Mar 11am–4:30pm Sat, Sun
1 Apr–30 Jun 11am–6pm Mon, Thu, Fri, Sat, Sun
1 Jul–31 Aug 11am–6pm Mon, Wed, Thu, Fri, Sat, Sun
1 Sep–17 Sep 11am–6pm Mon, Thu, Fri, Sat, Sun
20 Sep–28 Oct 11am–4:30pm Mon, Thu, Fri, Sat, Sun

Castle/museum
1 Apr–30 Jun 1pm–5pm Mon, Thu, Fri, Sat, Sun
1 Jul–31 Aug 1pm–5pm Mon, Wed, Thu, Fri, Sat, Sun
1 Sep–17 Sep 1pm–5pm Mon, Thu, Fri, Sat, Sun
20 Sep–28 Oct 1pm–4pm Mon, Thu, Fri, Sat, Sun

Restaurant/shop
17 Mar–31 Mar 11am–4:30pm Sat, Sun
1 Apr–30 Jun 11am–5:30pm Mon, Thu, Fri, Sat, Sun

The Argory

Historic house Garden Countryside

144 Derrycaw Road, Moy,
Dungannon, Co.
Armagh, BT71 6NA
028 8778 4753

OPENING TIMES

**House closed for
refurbishment during 2007**

Grounds
1 Mar–30 Apr 10am–4pm
Mon–Sun
1 May–30 Sep 10am–7pm
Mon–Sun

Tea-room/shop
17 Mar–30 Jun 2pm–6pm Sat,
Sun
1 Jul–31 Aug 2pm–6pm
Mon–Sun
1 Sep–30 Sep 2pm–6pm Sat,
Sun

A very imposing house (closed for refurbishment in 2007) from the 1820s, with lovely garden, woodlands and beautiful riverside walks. It's a real time capsule: not much has changed since 1900, when the Bond family lived there. There will be a lot of activities and information about the ongoing refurbishment, keep an eye out for the men in hard hats.

Wicked wildlife walks
The estate is over 300 acres and includes a range of beautiful walks, from the short to the more lengthy for those of you who really want to stretch your legs. If you wander down by the river, you may spot a kingfisher or a buzzard swooping over one of the fields. It is a haven for wildlife, see how many birds you can spot.

What to see
- A collection of carriages, but sorry, no horses!
- The acetylene gas plant (hint, they don't need watering…) in the stableyard.
- A sundial in the middle of the rose garden.

What to do
- Explore the swings, slides and other equipment in the playground, if you have any energy left after your walks.
- Visit the award-winning Lady Ada's tea-room – our cakes are second to none!
- Follow one of the walks round the estate (details available).

Special events
There are tons of exciting events all year round, including our Victorian Christmas Fayre, where you can enjoy music, festive food and perhaps even a visit from Santa. Other highlights include craft fairs, snowdrop walks and a French day.

By the way…
- Try the children's quiz trail. Changing facilities, and baby slings for hire.

Castle Ward

Historic house Mill Garden Park Farm Nature reserve

Here's a house that can't make up its mind – one façade is Classical and the other side is Gothic. In fact, Castle Ward is famous for its mix of architectural styles, inside and out, as well as the breathtaking views across Strangford Lough. Worth a visit in spring especially, for acres of bluebells.

Strangford Lough

From Castle Ward you can watch huge flocks of pale-bellied Brent Geese coming south over this huge seawater lake. There's a festival every autumn to celebrate their arrival. There are also seals and otters. The name means 'strong fjord', and the current is indeed very strong – look out for sailboats going backwards, or the ferry struggling against the current.

What to see

- Farm animals – including rare Irish moiled cattle; moiled means 'hornless'.
- Farm machinery in the farmyard.
- The basement and tunnel inside the house.
- See – and touch – all the interesting natural objects in the Wildlife Centre.

Strangford, Downpatrick,
Co. Down, BT30 7LS
028 4488 1204

OPENING TIMES

Grounds
1 Mar–31 Mar 10am–4pm
Mon–Sun
1 Apr–30 Sep 10am–8pm
Mon–Sun

House
17 Mar–19 Mar 1pm–6pm
Mon, Sat, Sun
1 Apr–28 May 1pm–6pm Sat,
Sun
1 Jun–30 Jun 1pm–6pm Mon,
Tue, Wed, Fri, Sat, Sun
1 Jul–31 Aug 12–6pm
Mon–Sun
1 Sep–30 Sep 1pm–6pm Sat,
Sun

Wales & Northern Ireland

continued… 151

What to do

- There's a playground for under-10s as well as a spectacular adventure playground for those with longer legs.
- Dress up and play with period toys in the Victorian Past Times Centre.
- Take a picnic or food for a barbecue, and play ball games on the lawns.

Special events

Family events include seasonal craft fairs, Santa's House, nature rambles, summer activity programme, summer kayak camp and much more.

By the way...

- There are many steps at the front; an alternative entrance has fewer. Wheelchairs can be booked.
- Baby-changing facilities and hip-carry seats for loan. There's a children's menu in the tea-room, too.

Crom

Park Countryside Nature reserve Wood Boat trip Wetland

If you fancy a spot of fishing, camping or would like to hire a boat to splosh around in a magical maze of water, peninsulas and islands, then Crom's your place. Set on the shores of Upper Lough Erne, this area is rightfully one of the Trust's most important nature reserves.

Wild about life
There are many rare species here, including pine martens, red squirrels and badgers. Put on good shoes and get back to nature. Or put on your best togs and get married – we're licensed for civil weddings, too.

What to see
- Wild garlic (pretty, not smelly), violets and rare mosses and lichens.
- The purple hairstreak butterfly
- Cormorants and curlews – listen out for the curlew's shrill cry.

What to do
- Arrange to stay overnight in the mammal hide to look out for pine martens.
- Wend your way around the islands in a hired boat, or ride through the reserve on the Kingfisher Trail cycle path.
- Explore one of the trails, or take a guided tour.

Special events
We have some summer events like small pet competitions and garden fairs; get in touch for more details. And don't forget – you can stay in our campsite, too.

By the way...
- Dogs on leads only, please, but welcome.
- The 19th-century castle you'll see is not open to the public. But our award-winning Visitor Centre and tea-room is, so do pop in.
- You can book our wheelchair, and the grounds have an accessible route.

Upper Lough Erne,
Newtownbutler,
Co. Fermanagh, BT92 8AP
028 6773 8118

OPENING TIMES
Grounds
17 Mar–1 Jun 10am–6pm
Mon–Sun
2 Jun–31 Aug 10am–7pm
Mon–Sun
1 Sep–30 Sep 10am–6pm
Mon–Sun

Visitor centre
17 Mar–1 Apr 10am–6pm Sat,
Sun
(Easter)
6 Apr–13 Apr 10am–6pm
Mon–Sun
14 Apr–29 Apr 10am–6pm Sat,
Sun
1 May–9 Sep 10am–6pm
Mon–Sun
15 Sep–30 Sep 10am–6pm
Sat, Sun

Notes
Campsite charge: £10 per tent per night

Florence Court

Historic house Garden Park

Enniskillen,
Co. Fermanagh, BT92 1DB
028 6634 8249

OPENING TIMES

Grounds
1 Mar–31 Mar 10am–4pm
Mon–Sun
1 Apr–30 Sep 10am–8pm
Mon–Sun
1 Oct–28 Feb 08 10am–4pm
Mon–Sun

House
17 Mar–19 Mar 1pm–6pm
Mon, Sat, Sun
1 Apr–28 May 1pm–6pm Sat,
Sun
1 Jun–30 Jun 1pm–6pm Mon,
Wed, Thu, Fri, Sat, Sun
1 Jul–31 Aug 12–6pm
Mon–Sun
1 Sep–30 Sep 1pm–6pm Sat,
Sun

Tea-room/shop
As house; Closes 5:30pm

One of Ulster's most important 18th-century houses, which used to be home to the Earls of Enniskillen. The setting is lovely, with the Cuilcagh mountains as a dramatic backdrop to the grounds, and a mill and a walled garden to explore. There's also a playground for smaller people's adventures.

That's a bit fishy...
William Willoughby Cole, 3rd Earl of Enniskillen (1807–1886) was a palaeontologist – he studied ancient rocks and fossils. He was particularly keen on collecting fossil fishes. Now they're in the Natural History Museum in London, although there are lots of other oddities in the house.

What to see
- The famous Florence Court Yew tree, supposed to be the 'parent' of all Irish yew trees.
- A hydraulic ram and water-powered saw-mill in the grounds.
- A blacksmith's forge, carpenter's workshop and an eel house. And an ice-house, from the days before fridges kept things cool.

What to do
- On Sundays in summer, go on one of our 'Living History Tours' to get a taste of life in the house.
- Swing and snack in the playground and picnic area.
- Try out the quiz and trail for younger members.

Special events
Summer weekends are a good time to find special family activities like children's fun days, craft shows and even Victorian fashion shows. And we have a spooky Halloween Craft Fayre with face-painting – and perhaps ghosts! Give us a call.

By the way...
- We have wheelchairs, and a ramp is available. The 1400-metre (¾-mile) path around the grounds is mostly very suitable for pushchairs or wheelchairs.
- Baby-changing and baby slings for loan.
- Dogs on leads, please.

Giant's Causeway

Rock formations   Walks

These rock formations really do look as if they were made for giants to stroll along. Discovered by the Bishop of Derry, in the 1600s, they have amazed visitors ever since. There are lovely paths to follow along the coastline, and the area is both an Area of Outstanding Natural Beauty and the only World Heritage Site in Northern Ireland.

Fee foe fie Finn

Legend has it the causeway was built by giant Finn McCool so he could walk to Scotland and fight Benandonner. Finn fell asleep on the way, and his clever wife put a blanket over him. When Benandonner came along she pretended Finn was her baby. Benandonner figured if that's the baby, his Dad must be pretty darned big, and ran off home! Actually the 40,000-odd basalt columns are the result of volcanic eruptions, over 60 million years ago. But even that is pretty amazing.

What to see

- Hexagonal (six-sided) stepping stones in the causeway. But can you see some that have five, seven or even eight sides?
- A video history of the Causeway.
- Lots of seabirds and other wildlife from the cliffs (but don't get too near the edge!)

What to do

- Follow the North Antrim Coastal path and read the info panels.
- If you walk far enough, you'll get to the Carrick-a-Rede rope bridge.
- Sit in the Wishing Chair rock and make a wish.

By the way...

- There's a ramped entrance to the visitor centre, and a wheelchair available.
- It's a good idea to wear good shoes if you're going to have a walk.
- Dogs on leads are welcome, as are pushchairs and baby-carriers. Tea-room, children's menu and baby-changing facilities.

44a Causeway Road,
Bushmills,
Co. Antrim, BT57 8SU
028 2073 1582

OPENING TIMES
All year Mon–Sun

Wales & Northern Ireland

Mount Stewart House

Historic house   Gardens   Temple of the Winds   Walks

Portaferry Road, Newtownards,
Co. Down, BT22 2AD
028 4278 8387

OPENING TIMES

Lakeside gardens
1 Mar–28 Feb 08 10–sunset
Mon–Sun

Formal gardens
17 Mar–31 Mar 10am–4pm
Sat, Sun
1 Apr–30 Apr 10am–6pm
Mon–Sun
1 May–30 Sep 10am–8pm
Mon–Sun
1 Oct–31 Oct 10am–6pm
Mon–Sun

House
17 Mar–29 Apr 12–6pm Sat,
Sun
2 May–31 May 1pm–6pm Mon,
Wed, Thu, Fri, Sat, Sun
1 Jun–30 Jun 1pm–6pm
Mon–Sun
1 Jul–31 Aug 12–6pm
Mon–Sun
1 Sep–30 Sep 1pm–6pm Mon,
Wed, Thu, Fri, Sat, Sun
6 Oct–28 Oct 12–6pm Sat, Sun

Lakeside gardens
1 Mar–28 Feb 08 10–sunset
Mon–Sun

The famous gardens here are among the best in the care of the National Trust, laid out in the 1920s by Lady Londonderry in a series of different garden rooms, or 'parterres'. There's something new around every corner, and many dramatic views. The house has world-famous paintings, including a very famous painting of a horse by George Stubbs, almost large as life. The socialite Londonderry family were great party-givers, and entertained many well-known politicians, including Winston Churchill. Stories and memorabilia abound in the house.

Animal magic
Lady Londonderry made all the politicians who visited members of her elite Ark Club. You can see animal pictures of them in the tearoom – Winston Churchill was 'Winnie the Warlock'. Wonder which animal today's prime minister would be?

What to see
- Dinosaurs in the garden, and a horse with a monkey on its back.
- Find 'Mairi Mairi quite contrary' sitting in the middle of a pond – with her cockle shells, of course, real banana trees.

What to do
- Creep down the underground tunnel by the Temple of the Winds.
- Find the crocodile and the dodo in the gardens.
- Picnic by the main gates and enjoy the view over Strangford Lough.

Special events
We have summer jazz concerts that all the family can enjoy, on the last Sunday of the month from April to September. Activities for smaller visitors include Dinosaur Day and Santa's Grotto. Get in touch to find what's on and book if necessary.

By the way...
- The entrance to the property is level and we have wheelchairs available, though you need to book.
- There's a special sensory trail in the gardens; ask for details at reception.
- We have baby-changing facilities and a children's menu in the restaurant.

Springhill and Wellbrook Beetling Mill
Historic house Garden Museum Mill

Wellbrook offers some lovely walks and picnic places by the Ballinderry River. The mill has its original hammer machinery, and demonstrations of the linen process by costumed guides. Down the road Springhill is an atmospheric house with an unusual and colourful costume exhibition.

No beetles were harmed in the making of this...
Beetling is actually the final stage in the production of linen, a very important industry in 19th-century Ireland. Hammer machinery was used to beat a sheen into the cloth. No beetles involved! Springhill has its own ghost, an award-winning costume collection and is known as the prettiest house in Ulster.

What to see
- At Springhill, Kentuck rifles and blunderbusses.
- A nursery packed with toys, and the excellent costume museum.
- At Wellbrook, 30 massive noisy hammers working the linen (ear plugs, please!)

What to do
- At Springhill, follow woodland walks and test your skill on the Children's Adventure Trail.
- Visit the shell house and the play area.
- At Wellbrook, have a go at beetling, and try out the spinning wheel – it's much harder than you think!

Special events
Easter Egg trails, Teddy Bears' Picnic in June.

By the way...
- At Springhill and Wellbrook, pushchairs and back-carriers are OK, and dogs on leads are welcome in the grounds. If steps are a problem, ask to use the alternative entrance at Springhill and a photography album for the first floor of the house. We can lend a wheelchair at Springhill. There's a handling collection at Wellbrook, and a guide available to talk to visitors. There are some steps involved in the house.

Springhill
20 Springhill Road,
Moneymore, Magherafelt,
Co. Londonderry, BT45 7NQ
028 8674 8210

Wellbrook Beetling Mill
20 Wellbrook Road,
Corkhill, Cookstown,
Co. Tyrone, BT80 9RY
028 8674 8210

OPENING TIMES
17 Mar–30 Jun 1pm–6pm Sat, Sun
1 Jul–31 Aug 12–6pm Mon–Sun
1 Sep–30 Sep 1pm–6pm Sat, Sun

Index

Joining the National Trust

Join the National Trust today and experience unlimited, free days out for all the family. Entertain and educate in some of Britain's most beautiful places, whilst helping to protect them for future generations.

Whether you and your family are interested in gardens, castles, wildlife, or places linked to famous events or people, National Trust family membership offers more than 300 historic houses and gardens, 700 miles of coastline and almost 250,000 hectares of stunning countryside, you'll never be short of exciting family days out.

As members of the National Trust, you'll not only have the benefits of free car parking and entry to our properties, you'll also receive a comprehensive membership pack, complete with our *Members' Handbook* – the complete guide to all our sites – a regional newsletter to keep you informed of all the National Trust events taking place in your area, and a useful Information booklet, which will answer all your membership questions. You'll also receive a copy of our beautifully illustrated *Members' Magazine* three times a year. All this for as little as 15p a day*.

Family Group (2006 rate*: £73)
For two adults living at the same address, and their children and grandchildren under 18.

Family one adult (2006 rate*: £55)
For one adult and his/her children under 18, living at the same address.

To join, simply visit www.nationaltrust.org.uk or phone 0870 458 4000, quoting the following unique code: NT060077M1.

*Rates current to 28th February 2007.

NATIONAL TRUST FAMILY PROGRAMME

🌿 THE NATIONAL TRUST

family

sky

programme sponsor

Our family programme sponsor Sky continues to support our exciting range of family events throughout 2007 in England, Wales and Northern Ireland – attracting a new generation of visitors to the Trust. Come and hunt for chocolate eggs at our Easter trails, pack a picnic for outdoor family theatre and have a spooky time at the Halloween events.

BRING A FRIEND FOR FREE

This coupon entitles one person to free entry (once only) to any one of the participating National Trust properties when accompanied by a paying adult from 13 April 2007 and 25 May 2007. (See terms & conditions for further details)

TITLE _____ FIRST NAME _____

SURNAME _____

ADDRESS _____

_____

POSTCODE _____

VISIT DATE _____

The National Trust collects and processes personal information for the purposes of customer analysis and direct marketing so that we can contact you about our conservation, membership, fundraising and other activities. Please tick this box if you would prefer not to hear from |the National Trust in this way ❑

THE NATIONAL TRUST

FREE CHILDREN'S MEAL VOUCHER

Please complete in block capitals. This voucher is ONLY valid on completion of name and address details. This voucher entitles one person to a free children's meal when purchasing any adult main course over £4.95, at any one of the participating National Trust properties (see separate list) during March and April 2007.

TITLE _____ FIRST NAME _____

SURNAME_____

ADDRESS _____

_____

POSTCODE_____EMAIL _____

VISIT DATE _____

CODE NT060017V3 SITE CODE _____

(for office use only).

The National Trust collects and processes personal information for the purposes of customer analysis and direct marketing so that we can contact you about our conservation, membership, fundraising and other activities. Please tick this box if you would prefer not to hear from the National Trust in this way ❑

THE NATIONAL TRUST

CHILDREN GO FREE WITH
THE NATIONAL TRUST

This coupon entitles up to 2 children (under 16) free entry (once only) to any one of the participating National Trust properties when accompanied by a paying adult from 10 September 2007 until 26 October 2007. (See terms & conditions for further details)

TITLE _____ FIRST NAME _____

SURNAME _____

ADDRESS_____

_____

POSTCODE _____

VISIT DATE _____

The National Trust collects and processes personal information for the purposes of customer analysis and direct marketing so that we can contact you about our conservation, membership, fundraising and other activities. Please tick this box if you would prefer not to hear from the National Trust in this way ❑

THE NATIONAL TRUST

SPEND £15 OR MORE IN A
NATIONAL TRUST SHOP
AND SAVE £2

Terms and conditions

Offer available only at National Trust shops on production of this voucher. This excludes NT admission, membership, gift vouchers, mail order and catering purchases. This voucher cannot be used in conjunction with any other offers or exchanged for cash.

Offer ends 31 Dec 2007.

THE NATIONAL TRUST